A HISTORY

OF THE

GREAT NORTH OF SCOTLAND RAILWAY

Printed in Great Britain:
R. Tilling, 106 Great Dover Street, London, S.E.1.

A History

of the

Great North of Scotland Railway

By

Sir MALCOLM BARCLAY-HARVEY, K.C.M.G.

LONDON:

THE LOCOMOTIVE PUBLISHING CO., LIMITED,

3 AMEN CORNER, E.C.4.

1940

From an Oil Painting by F. Moore

THE DEESIDE EXPRESS

CONTENTS.

LIST OF PLATES

LIST OF TEXT ILLUSTRATIONS.

PREFACE.

The North East corner of Scotland consisting of the counties of Aberdeen, Banff and Moray, is mainly an agricultural district and, except for its river valleys and coasts, not one which is likely to attract a large number of tourists. The Great North of Scotland Railway which served it was therefore not known to such a wide circle as most of the other Scottish Railways. Moreover, despite strenuous efforts it never quite succeeded in overcoming early mistakes and making itself a through route to the North so had to rely chiefly on local traffic. Despite all this it gave a lead in a surprising number of ways and was, at least during one period of its life, easily the best of all the smaller British Railways. The first half century of its life was an almost continuous battle with adversity or its neighbours and the history both of that period and that of the quieter years that followed is much too interesting to be allowed to pass into the limbo of things forgotten. This book has therefore been written to tell the story of that pugnacious and courageous little railway in the hope and belief that it is of more than local interest.

I must confess to having had considerable difficulty in getting at the truth about some of the early doings of the railway owing to contradictory evidence. Like others in a similar predicament I have taken the evidence of those whom I considered the most reliable witnesses. Great help was given me in this task by Mr. David Stewart of Banchory Devenick, who most kindly lent me some notes on the rail-

B

way's history in the "fifties" and "sixties" of last century, which helped me greatly in the task of unravelling the tangled story of those years. To this source I am also indebted for the information about the other users of the title "Great North of Scotland Railway."

Much of the history of these and other periods has been gleaned from evidence given before many Parliamentary Committees, and I am greatly indebted to Miss Court, Accountant of the House of Lords, who has given me much courteous assistance in these researches.

My most grateful thanks are also due to many others who have given me much valuable help. To the late Mr. George Davidson who kindly gave me access to the early Minute Books of the Company many years ago, to Mr. James B. Singer, the Traffic Superintendent of the Northern Scottish Area of the London & North Eastern Railway, to whom I am indebted for most courteously supplying me with much information and several of the illustrations which appear in this book; also to Mr. T. E. Heywood, the Locomotive Superintendent of the Northern Area of the London & North Eastern Railway, who has also kindly helped me with my chapter on rolling stock and supplied me with some of the illustrations; and Mr. Hugh Gordon who has also helped me greatly about the locomotives. Major S. A. Forbes, too, has been most kind in assisting me to find a way through the intricacies of the history of the early locomotives and particularly that of the three small independent Companies—the Deeside, the Morayshire and the Banffshire, and Mr. A. C. W. Lowe in reading the proofs and making some most useful suggestions. To the North British Locomotive Company I am also grateful for the illustrations of some of the locomotives built by them. Last, but by no means least, my grateful thanks are also due to General Sir James Burnett, Bart., of Leys, for information about the early history of the Queen's Messenger trains.

I must also acknowledge my indebtedness to " Neele's Railway Reminiscences" for information about Queen Victoria's earlier journeys to Balmoral; to G. M. Fraser's "Old Deeside Road" for some of the information about the early Deeside railway; to Pratt's "British Railways and the Great War" for most of the information about the Great North's war work; to H. A. Vallance's History of the Highland Railway; to the Editor of the Stephenson Locomotive Society's Bulletin for the illustrations from Mr. Ward's drawings, and to many articles in " The Locomotive " and "The Railway Magazine", particularly those by the late E. L. Ahrons, to which I am indebted for some of the more technical details of the early locomotives.

When I began writing this book, now nearly seventeen years ago, I had no idea it would take so long to complete. Other work, however, monopolised my time, and it has only been during short intervals in the intervening years that I have been able to do any work on it. That work has been to me a most interesting one, and if the book gives even a small percentage of that interest to its readers, I shall be more than rewarded for the labours of writing it.

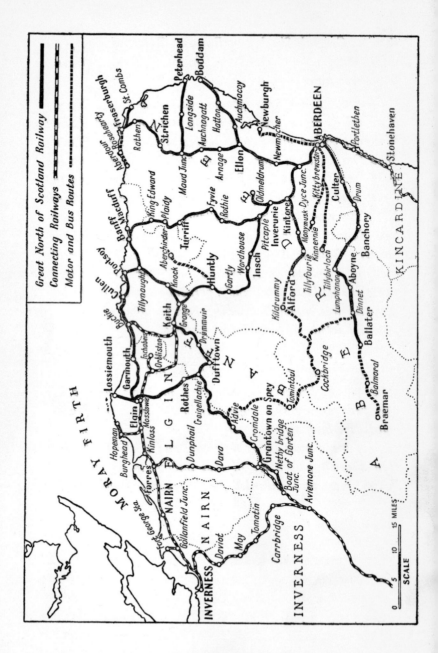

Great North of Scotland Railway

Connecting Railways

Motor and Bus Routes

CHAPTER ONE.

BEGINNINGS.

THE City and Royal Burgh of Aberdeen is one of more than respectable antiquity. It is by a long way the most Northerly of the very large cities and it may well be asked how such a large town comes to exist so far from the main centres of production and in a district devoid of almost all mineral wealth. One answer might be that it is the result of a prodigious capacity for collecting "saxpences" on the part of its population but this explanation, though possibly a popular one, would certainly be superficial. After all, saxpences have to be earned before they can be collected! The true answer is that its existence and prosperity were made possible by the energy and business capacity of its inhabitants.

That being so it is rather strange that it should have been so long before any step was taken in the matter of railway development, for it was not till 1844 that the first serious proposal for a railway to serve Aberdeen was made. Naturally enough, this was for a line to connect the city with other railways then made or in the course of construction farther South, so to give rail connection with the main centres of population. There were three rival projects, one of which was called the "Great North of Scotland Railway" and this name was used for the first time on its prospectus dated April 23rd, 1844. This railway, however, failed to get the sanction of Parliament and nothing more was heard of it.

The first of the two other schemes—which had appeared before this Great North of Scotland—was to be called the Aberdeen, Perth and Dundee Railway and was to run from Aberdeen through the Vale of Strathmore to Perth, connecting with the already completed Arbroath and Forfar and Dundee and Newtyle Railways. On leaving Aberdeen it was to follow the North Bank of the Dee as far as a point opposite Durris and then turn South by way of Glenbervie, Auchenblae and Laurencekirk to Montrose, Brechin and the South. In its original prospectus it was suggested that it should be worked on the atmospheric system "as had been successfully done in the case of the Dublin and Kingstown Railway", and by using this system a saving of 40 per cent. in working expenses was expected.

A rival scheme appeared immediately after to pass through Stonehaven, Johnshaven and Montrose to Arbroath, or alternately to a junction with the Arbroath and Forfar line at Friockheim.   This latter was to be known as the Aberdeen and East Coast Railway and followed much more closely the route taken by the turnpike road, which had early in the century replaced the very ancient "Causey Mouth" highway to the South. But the rivals came to an understanding very quickly, and on April 3rd, 1844, a notice addressed to the Proprietors of the Counties of Aberdeen, Banff, Moray and Inverness appeared in the local Press to the effect that a joint survey of the lines to the South had been agreed upon, and that a survey was also to be made by Messrs. John Gibb & Co. of a line from Aberdeen to Inverness with branches to Peterhead and Banff. A fortnight later a prospectus of the "Aberdeen Railway" appeared, being a compromise between these two schemes for the southern line. This scheme was duly proceeded with and its promoters were successful in getting powers to construct their line by an Act which received Royal Assent on July 31st, 1845.

In the meantime steps had been taken with regard to the Inverness line. On March 30th, 1844, a letter was sent out to the landowners in the district asking them to give facilities to the engineers for making a survey of the route, and in May of that year instructions were given to Mr. Gibb, the engineer, to prepare such a survey of the best route. This was completed early in the following year and a preliminary Prospectus was drawn up dated 4th February, 1845, which announced the formation of a Company to be known as the Great North Railway, to build a line from Aberdeen to Inverness, having a capital of £1,100,000 divided into 22,000 shares of £50. each. The Railway was to commence at the Aberdeen Railway's station in Aberdeen and to proceed by way of old Aberdeen and the River Don to Inverurie and thence by Oyne, Premnay, Insch, Gartly and Huntly to Avochie, where the River Deveron was to be crossed. From there it would pass along Strath Isla and through Fyfe Keith, crossing the River Spey at Boat of Bridge, and then to follow what is practically the course of the present line of the London, Midland and Scottish Railway through Elgin, Forres and

Nairn to Inverness. Branches were to be given off to Banff and to Portsoy from a junction in Strath Isla, to Speymouth from a junction at the crossing place over the Spey, to Lossiemouth or Burghhead from a junction near Elgin, and to Fort George from Nairn.

The dividend prospects were clearly considered to be rosy; the estimated receipts, which were based upon observations made during the months of October and November, being passengers £67,500, and goods £48,000—Total £115,500, while working expenses were only allowed at the rate of one-third of this total. On this computation a dividend of 7 per cent. was anticipated, but better was hoped for as traffic in the summer months would be greater than during the autumn, on which basis these figures had been fixed.

On March 3rd a meeting was held "within the writing chambers of Messrs. Adam & Anderson, Advocates in Aberdeen", at which a preliminary Committee of twelve was appointed to promote the undertaking. A prospectus was issued in Aberdeen dated March 8th and another slightly different one in London on March 20th. This latter was headed :—

GREAT
NORTH OF SCOTLAND RAILWAY
FROM
ABERDEEN TO INVERNESS
IN CONTINUATION OF THE ABERDEEN LINE
FROM THE SOUTH.

The capital was to be the same as that mentioned in the preliminary prospectus but the new one held out even better prospects than the former. Passenger

Traffic was now estimated at £98,303 and Goods at £76,413, making a total of £174,716, and again allowing working expenses at 33⅓% of the total income. The net revenue was put at £116,478 "equal to a dividend on the estimated cost of upwards of 10 per cent". A list of the Provisional Committee was given, which included the Earl of Errol, Lord Lieutenant of Aberdeenshire, the Earl of Moray, Lord Lieutenant of Morayshire, Sir R. D. H. Elphinstone, Mr. Thomas Blaikie, Lord Provost of Aberdeen, Mr. Alexander Mactavish, City Clerk of Inverness, and a large number of other influential people from the whole district which it was proposed to serve. Mr. William Cubitt was to be the Consulting Engineer and Mr. Alexander Gibb the acting engineer. The proposed Railway was the same as that suggested in the preliminary prospectus except that the Fort George branch was dropped.

Thus was the Great North of Scotland Railway introduced to the world. The scheme put forward was a logical and comprehensive one for serving the North East of Scotland. and it was well received. So far indeed all had been plain sailing and the hour must have seemed a most propitious one for promoting a Railway. In the year 1845 the Railway mania reached its height. Money for railway schemes was practically to be had for the asking and the Great North scheme shared in the general enthusiasm. At a meeting on 31st March of that year it was reported that there had already been 75,000 applications for the 22,000 shares exclusive of the London and Glasgow lists! No wonder that the report said "There can be no doubt that a selection of a wealthy and influential Proprietary can be made from among the numerous applicants". Great difficulty was experienced in making this selection but it was finally decided to allot 25 per cent. more shares than were required in order to cover those not taken up. Altogether 27,776 were allotted and 27,415 taken up. At this meeting the first directors were appointed, with Lord Provost Blaikie as Convener, to allot stock and carry out details of the undertaking. It is interesting to note that thus early they were empowered to arrange for the amalgamation of the Great North with the Aberdeen Railway if they thought fit, and this step was actually decided upon at a meeting in September of that year. As the two Companies had largely been promoted by the same people and had several directors in common they were naturally at that time working very closely together.

In order to eliminate a possible rival the directors hit on the idea of buying up the Aberdeenshire Canal. This canal had been made to connect Port Elphinstone on the River Don near Inverurie with Aberdeen harbour. The first proposals for its construction were made in 1795, but it did not come into use until twelve years later and direct access to the harbour was only obtained in 1834. Up till then the terminal basin had been on the site of what is now the Waterloo Goods Station. It was 18¼ miles long and cost £44,500 to make, John Rennie being the engineer. Passengers were conveyed in "Flyboats" drawn by two horses in tandem and they managed to achieve a speed of eight miles an hour; goods were conveyed on the Company's barges, of which there were seventeen, which were let out to the consignors

THE CANAL BRANCH.

of the goods who supplied their own horses. In all there were seventeen locks, of which fourteen were between Kittybrewster and the harbour. Though it cannot be said for certain, it is probable that the heavy retaining wall shown in the illustration of the Waterloo branch of the railway was originally a wall of one of those locks.

This canal was not a financial success and had never paid any dividend. But in 1844 it had earned £2,553 16s. 4d. with a total expenditure of £1,337 0s. 7½d. An offer of £36,000 was made for it, which, after some negotiation, was accepted. By an unfortunate mistake the purchase of the Canal was not regularized by getting Parliamentary authority as it should have been for the Canal was a Statutory undertaking. As a result of this omission the Railway had to compensate anyone whose interests were affected by the closing of the Canal and this cost them a further ten thousand pounds.

Another type of opponent had also to be faced in the Road Trustees. The County of Aberdeen had built a large number of roads under the Turnpike Road Acts of the late eighteenth and early nineteenth century, and considerable sums of money had been spent, the interest on which was looked for from the tolls. At this time the total surplus revenue from the Aberdeenshire Roads which would be affected by the building of a Railway—including the Deeside and Alford roads—was £3,424 per annum. Prolonged negotiations took place with the Aberdeenshire authorities before an agreement could be reached, though one was quickly come to with Banffshire.

By the autumn of 1845 the consulting engineers had approved the acting engineer's plans, and a Bill was promoted for the session of 1846. Then followed a fierce Parliamentary contest for the Great North was not the only scheme put forward for a railway to Inverness. The inhabitants of the Highland capital wanted a more direct route to the south than one by way of Aberdeen and were proposing to built a railway from Inverness to Perth following the great Highland road, and this railway at its first appearance was also given the title of Great North of Scotland. They also proposed a line to Elgin through Nairn and Forres. The first of these schemes soon changed its name to the Perth and Inverness Railway, and shortly before the last date for depositing plans with the Board of Trade these two Inverness schemes were amalgamated.

There was also another rival called the Aberdeen, Banff and Elgin which would have gone north to Banff and then along the coast to Elgin, with branches to Peterhead and Fraserburgh, which, however, were not included in its bill. At Elgin it would have connected with the Inverness and Elgin line. Lastly, as will be told later, there was the Morayshire line, but that was not a rival.

The Great North won its Parliamentary battle and on June 26th, 1846, its Bill received the Royal Assent and the Great North of Scotland Railway was duly incorporated. In July of the same year Acts were passed for the construction of an Alford Valley line, and the Great North of Scotland (Eastern extension) Railway, being a line from Dyce to Fraserburgh with a branch from Stewartfield to Peterhead—both in reality branches of the Great North.

The victory had been dearly bought—it cost the victorious Company £50,000. Amongst other items a sum of £126 13s. od. is mentioned as having been spent on the entertainment of witnesses at Greenwich on the passing of the Bill, and two opponents were bought off at a total cost of £1,360!

This large total frightened the shareholders who were now unwilling to go on with their railway. Moreover, the Railway fever which reached its crisis in 1845 had burnt itself out and by the time the Great North Bill had become an Act the whole financial situation had changed. So far now were the directors from being able to make a selection of "wealthy and influential" shareholders that they were not even in a position to raise the money to commence making the line. And so in their first report they guardedly recommended the postponement of the works "for fear of the effect on the money and labour market of the diversion of so much Capital to Railway work". They suggested waiting to see how the Aberdeen Railway fared before launching forth their own scheme, and this policy was agreed to by the shareholders at the first ordinary meeting held on August 21st, 1846. At the same meeting it was decided to fix the Directors' fees at one hundred pounds per annum, the Auditors' salary at ten guineas each, and the Secretary's salary at one hundred pounds per annum. The smallness of the amounts was due to the fact that to begin with very little work was anticipated.

An Act for the amalgamation of the Aberdeen and Great North Railways was passed in 1847 which was to become operative when half of the capital of each was paid up and expended on their lines   It provided that the Aberdeen Railway was to be purchased or leased by the Great North of Scotland which was to be the title of the combined Company. However, the next two years passed without any progress being made by the northern Company and during that time the two drew gradually apart.   In 1848 a radical change was made in the Aberdeen Company's Board of Directors, so one of the principal ties which had originally bound them was broken.   In addition, the Great North were alarmed at the increasing cost of the Aberdeen line and there had also been a good deal of disagreement about the site of the proposed joint station.

The Aberdeen Railway had originally intended to come into Aberdeen from Ferryhill by a high viaduct to a station just east of Market Street and ground for a station was bought between the Market and Guild Streets.   (Some of the arches of the viaduct had actually been built and had to be pulled down when it was decided to have the station on a lower level.)   The Great North, by its Act of 1846, would have entered the city by Berryden, come down by the west side of Union Bridge passing under Union Street by a cutting and joined the Aberdeen line at a point just south of where the present Aberdeen Joint Station stands. As this junction would have faced south the Great North trains would have had to back from it into the terminus, which was a little to the north east of the junction.

In 1850 the Aberdeen line abandoned this plan and got powers to build a station below Guild Street and on a lower level, arrangements being made at the same time for the alteration to the junction with the Great North. The site chosen for a station was not a good one, being too small, and was considered to be too far from the centre of the town, so in 1852 the Great North took the feu on which the Palace Hotel now stands with the intention of making a station there, to which the Aberdeen Railway could also come if they were so minded. But in the end they decided to start from Kittybrewster, so nothing came of this scheme.

Early in 1849 the directors came to the conclusion that something must be done towards the construction of their line. Powers to prolong the time allowed for construction of the railway had already been obtained and advantage was now taken of a journey to London of one of the directors to sound the Duke of Richmond —the largest landowner in their district—as to his attitude towards the Railway. He promised to do all he could to assist and he maintained this helpful attitude throughout the negotiations which followed, and it was largely owing to his assistance that the Railway was ever made. The Great North does not seem to have experienced any great difficulty in their dealings with landowners. Active steps were commenced for the purchase of land in August and subsequent negotiations seem to have been of a very amicable nature, landowners generally accepting the system of taking an annual feu duty in place of a capital sum for the land required.

At the same time tenders for the construction of the line in sections were called for from Mr. Brassey, the

well-known Railway Constructor, Mr. George Milne
and Messrs. Mitchell & Deans. The last named firm's
offer being the lowest and their tender having been
approved by the Company's Consulting Engineer at
the fourth General Meeting of the Company, held on
November 28th, 1849, on the unanimous recommen-
dation of the directors the shareholders agreed to
enter into a contract with that firm for the work to
proceed. The contract was to be for the whole line
but the Company were to have the right to stop at
Keith if they wished, as in fact they proposed to do.
Nevertheless in the event of their being able to complete the line before their powers expired the contract
was to hold good for such a continuation. The contractors agreed to take up one quarter of the Railway
Stock.

The estimated cost for a single line to Keith but with
works for a double one was £470,000, and in order
that the shareholders should have an idea how the
estimated cost of their line compared with that of
other Companies the following figures were quoted:

Cost per mile of Aberdeen Railway	...	£26,000
Caledonian	...	30,000
Dundee and Perth	...	20,000
Scottish Central	...	27,000
Edinburgh, Perth and Dundee	...	28,000
Glasgow and Ayr	...	25,000
Scottish Midland	...	20,000

The financial situation, however, was still very difficult. The next year was spent in efforts to obtain a
guarantee of one-fourth of the stock which was neces-

sary before a start could be made, and to raise money to oppose the Aberdeen Railway's Bill. For the Great North, as has already been told, disliked the plan for altering their approach to Aberdeen and the situation of their terminus, and they succeeded in getting modifications made in it. The Bill also contained provisions for repealing the amalgamation scheme of the Great North and Aberdeen Railways to which the Great North agreed, and which were therefore passed unopposed.

But money was not forthcoming and at the next General Meeting held in November, 1850, a proposal was made to reduce their capital and split the shares into smaller quantities. Powers were duly obtained to do this, and in 1851 the Company was practically re-formed. The Capital was reduced to £1,107,440, divided into postponed shares, i.e., those of the original subscribers and calls on shares issued before 1851, and preference shares which were new shares issued thereafter. The share value in each case was £10. The preference shares were to receive dividends up to 5 per cent., and any surplus beyond that was to go to the postponed shares. There was a virtually new Board of Directors though Sir James Elphinstone, who had become Chairman in 1849, continued in this office. Most of the shareholders, too, were different people from the original subscribers.

Negotiations were at that time entered into with the Aberdeen Railway with a view to inducing the shareholders of that concern to invest in the Great North. After a thorough examination of the Great North's position the Aberdeen directors agreed to recommend

c

their shareholders to do so. These negotiations, however, fell through, the Great North declaring that the
Aberdeen Railway insisted on terms but were unwilling to give any money, while the Aberdeen replied
that they were prepared to give the money but the
Great North would not agree to the terms!

There were also some curious negotiations with the
East Coast Companies—the Great Northern, York,
Newcastle and Berwick, and North British. Apparently these companies offered to subscribe £150,000
on condition that the Great North routed all traffic
by their lines which was not specially routed by the
West Coast route. The agreement was to last for an
unstated number of years and after that until the
Great North's ordinary dividend was five per cent.
for three consecutive years. The holders of shares so
raised were to get the dividend paid on Great North
preference shares with as much as possible added to
make up to five per cent. The Great North offered in
reply fifty per cent. of the profits on all their traffics
originating North of Aberdeen. It was hoped that by
this agreement it would be possible to construct their
line to Elgin, which was impossible without some such
assistance. However, nothing came of these suggestions despite long negotiations.

Some money was at last forthcoming and in the
autumn of 1852 the directors felt that a start could
be made. As, however, only £400,000 worth of
shares could be sold it was decided only to make a
line from Kittybrewster to Huntly. The contract for
the construction of the line had already been signed
in the previous year, so a start could be made at once.

COMMENCEMENT OF THE NORTH OF SCOTLAND RAILWAY, AT WESTHALL, ABERDEENSHIRE.

The ceremony of cutting the first sod was performed by Lady Elphinstone, wife of Sir James Elphinstone, the Chairman of the Company, at Westhall, near Oyne, on November 25th, 1852. There was a great company of people to witness the ceremony, (many of whom had come from Aberdeen in carriages decorated with railway signals!) and the occasion was one of much rejoicing. At the dinner which followed the Chairman, Sir James Elphinstone, said that it would be the policy of the Company to maintain communication with the harbour of Aberdeen and in furtherance of this policy the directors had decided to make a branch to the South side of the harbour from the proposed line, giving a junction with the Aberdeen railway.

Though there were no serious engineering works between Kittybrewster and Huntly some delay was caused in the construction of the line by the fact that cuttings at Logie-Elphinstone, Pitcaple and Fintray, and the embankment and cutting at Drakewells proved heavier than had been expected, but these delays do not seem to have been serious.

A more serious delay was caused by the canal. As has already been seen, it had been bought by the Railway before they got their Act of Incorporation but it was still being worked by the Canal Company on their behalf, and they thus got the interest on the purchase price. In order to keep the canal in use as long as possible the further portion of the railway was made first, but an arrangement was come to for the contractor to get the canal when he required it for making the railway. This he would do as the line ran close to it in many places, and actually on it for part of its length. When this time came the final arrangements for the transfer of the canal to the railway had not been completed for it had been decided that a general transfer was not possible but that each individual shareholder must sign his own transfer. The law agents of the two Companies kept the business to themselves, and as it involved much writing this caused a great deal of delay. Being impatient to get on with the work, the Contractor cut the bank of the canal and let the water out into the River Don before all these formalities had been completed. The result was that all the barges that were on the canal at the time were stranded and before they could be got to their destinations the break in the bank had to be made good and the canal refilled with water !

Further delays were also caused by the particularly severe weather experienced in the year 1853, but all these difficulties were successfully overcome and an engine passed over the whole line on August 31st, 1854. The line was opened to goods traffic on September 12th, and was formally opened on September 19th, 1854.

The opening was performed with due ceremony. A train consisting of twenty-five carriages hauled by two engines carrying four hundred people, including the directors and officials of the Company, left Aberdeen at eleven o'clock and reached Huntly in two hours. Crowds assembled all along the line to watch the train's progress, which was in accordance with its schedule. At Huntly a large marquee had been erected in a field near the station in which a dinner was given, presided over by the Duke of Richmond, who proposed the toast of the Great North of Scotland Railway and its further extension to the North. In his reply, the Chairman thanked the Duke for all the services he had rendered to the Company and also the proprietors along the line, many of whom, he said, had given their land for a feu duty and all of whom had accepted a recompense more moderate than had ever before been received for such an undertaking.

After the dinner was over the Aberdeen passengers returned to the train, which left Huntly at five o'clock and reached Aberdeen at seven, both outward and homeward journeys having been made punctually and without a hitch. The rolling stock commended itself to the reporter who described the carriages as "elegant and commodious" and reported further that the journey had been a very smooth one.

The line thus opened was thirty-nine and a half miles long and single throughout with very few crossing places. There were to be thirteen or fourteen intermediate stations though all of these were not ready at the time of opening. All still remain, except Buchanstone, between Oyne and Insch. There was not much to justify the title of " **Great** North of Scotland " in those days !

On leaving Kittybrewster the line follows the valley of the Don for about fourteen miles to Port Elphinstone, the terminus of the old canal. Here the river turns away sharply to the West and is crossed by the railway which thus gets to Inverurie. From Inverurie the line follows the course of the Urie for about six miles, turning westwards with it at Pitcaple. After

leaving the Urie it continues in a westerly direction
to get through a pass in the hills between Kennethmont and Gartly, and so into the valley of the Bogie
which it follows down to Huntly.

For the first four miles or so to Dyce the line is
on a rising gradient, though not a very steep one, but
from there nearly to Inveramsay it is almost level.
Here begins a long and trying bank to the summit
just short of Kennethmont—twelve miles in all, much
of which was as steep as 1 in 100 and only broken by
two short falls—one of about three-quarters of a mile,
beginning at what is now the twenty-fifth mile post,
and the other of rather more than a mile, ending just
beyond Insch station. This makes a very difficult
climb for heavy northbound trains. From the summit,
which is about 600 feet above sea level, there is a continuous fall to Huntly, which includes about a mile
at 1 in 100 near its start and much after that at 1 in
200 or steeper.

The line from Huntly to Keith was not opened till
two years later, but its general characteristics may ap-
propriately be considered here as it, together with the
Southern extension from Kittybrewster to Waterloo,
completed the original Great North of Scotland, the
other branches having been made by nominally
independent companies. Just north of Huntly the
Bogie falls into the Deveron and the railway follows
that river for about four miles to Avochie, where it
crosses it. Originally this crossing was made by a
single line stone bridge which can still be seen just
down stream of the present bridge, which was built
when the line was doubled in 1900. To this point

and for about a mile after the river is crossed the fall is almost continuous at gradients varying from 1 in 120 to 1 in 180, so that up-trains have a thirteen and a half mile bank to tackle which is mostly steeper than 1 in 200 and finishes with a mile at 1 in 100—a formidable task for heavy trains. Soon after leaving the Deveron the railway enters the flat valley of the Isla which it follows all the way to Keith at faintly rising gradients.

Keith Junction, where the Great North and Inverness and Aberdeen Junction railways joined, is situated just outside the town of Keith, but the site met with general approval as it served the whole district well. It was never an ornament to the countryside or a credit to its owners, but despite all its shortcomings managed to escape the rebuilding which transformed so many Great North stations later in its life and still continues to represent the sort of station which was considered good enough for passengers in the middle of last century.

The regular service was started on the day after the formal opening and the passenger train service was announced as follows :—

GREAT NORTH OF SCOTLAND RAILWAY.

Opening for Public Traffic.

On and after September 20th, 1854, and until further notice Trains will be run as under.

Down Trains	Goods	Passenger	Pssgr. & Parly.	Pssgr. & Mail
	a.m.	a.m.	p.m.	p.m.
Trains will not leave Kittybrewster before 5.15		8.35	1.30	6.30
Or reach Huntly before	8.57	10.35	3.30	8.30

Up Trains	Mixed & Mail	Passenger	Pssgr. & Parly.	Passenger
Trains will not leave	a m.	a.m.	a.m.	p.m.
Huntly before	4.25	6.15	11.0	4.0
Or arrive in Aberdeen before	7.25	8.15	1.0	6.0

A service of three coaches each way daily was maintained between Huntly and Inverness.

The passenger fares were fixed at 1¾d. a mile 1st class, 1¼d. a mile 3rd class, and 1d. a mile Parliamentary. A schedule of goods rates was published but caused much dissatisfaction as the rates were too high. They were therefore modified but even so were considerably higher than those on other Scottish lines.

At the start there were great difficulties owing to shortage of rolling stock. Out of twelve engines ordered, only six had been delivered, out of forty passenger carriages only twenty-four, and out of three hundred and fifty-six other vehicles only one hundred and sixty. Particularly serious for the railway serving an agricultural district was the fact that only one out of sixty cattle wagons had arrived. The builders of the carriages, Messrs. Brown, Marshall & Co. of Birmingham, said they had not expected the line to open so soon as their previous experience showed there was usually a delay of two months. The signals also proved unsatisfactory and more had to be ordered.

In consequence of all this there was great unpunctuality and, more serious still, there was a fatal accident within a week of the opening of the line. On the morning of September 23rd the train due at 8.15

a.m. was only arriving at nine o'clock owing to delays before starting from Huntly. It was the custom in those early days for incoming trains to stop just inside the distant signal about half a mile from the station and here the engine was taken off and run round to the back of the train which it then pushed in. On this occasion, however, the train failed to stop and, despite the fact that the driver reversed his engine, ran on and crashed into a train full of passengers which was awaiting its arrival in the station. This train had no engine attached so the first carriage had to withstand the full force of the impact and was completely smashed. One woman who was sitting beside her husband was killed on the spot, as when the carriage in which she was sitting was smashed she fell onto the line and was run over by the oncoming engine. In addition twenty-two other people were injured, two or three of them seriously. It was an unfortunate start, but the Great North's subsequent record in the matter of accidents was a very good one.

Kittybrewster was not an ideal site for a terminus as it was on the northern outskirts of the city and gave no connection with either the railway to the South or to the harbour. The idea of a rail connection with the southern line which had been an integral part of the original scheme, was not proceeded with, largely on account of its cost, but to keep the promise of the Chairman at the ceremony of the cutting of the first sod in 1852, powers had been obtained to make a railway down the bed of the old canal to Waterloo Quay. It was originally intended to continue this line to the South side of the docks, but this

proposal roused so much opposition from the harbour
trustees and the Aberdeen Railway that it was
dropped.   As a compromise the Harbour Trustees
agreed to lay rails along the docks between the Waterloo and Guild Street Stations—mainly apparently to
accommodate the cattle traffic which at that time
amounted to 50,000 head per annum. The branch to
Waterloo was opened for goods traffic on September
29th, 1855, and for passengers on April 1st, 1856. It
was known at that time as the Canal Branch as it was
entirely on the track of the old canal and the Waterloo station was built on the old canal basin near the
harbour.

The passenger station at Waterloo was a wooden
erection. To judge by present appearances the main
platform must have been very narrow and inconvenient—but the Great North of those days did not
study the convenience of its passengers very greatly.
The exterior view of the station is shown in the
illustration, the stone building at the end being the
old offices of the railway. They too were small,
cramped and ill lit and once the Denburn line and
joint station were opened they must have been
inconveniently far away from the Company's main
operations.

A terminus at Waterloo was certainly better than
one at Kittybrewster and it was admirably situated for
transfer of traffic to the docks, but it suffered from the
grave objection that it was nearly half a mile from
the Aberdeen and Deeside Railway Station at Guild
Street, and this separation of the stations was naturally
the cause of much inconvenience to the public and

WATERLOO STATION AND OFFICES.

ultimately much trouble to the railway company itself.

In two respects the Great North was unique from its opening—it was the only railway to be opened, equipped with electric telegraph throughout its whole length, and it had no second class carriages. Many years later it was followed, in this respect by the Midland on the advice of its Chairman, Mr. Ellis, who, during a visit to Aberdeenshire in 1872, had been so impressed by the saving of coaches on such occasions as cattle shows, etc., that he decided to recommend to his directors that they should follow the Great North's example—which they did.

To get an understanding of the future railway history of the North East of Scotland it is now necessary to turn back a little. The Great North having been long in coming, the people of Inverness got tired of waiting and decided to make a start on their own. A Bill was accordingly introduced in the session of 1854 for the construction of a line from Inverness to Nairn to be known as the Inverness and Nairn Railway. As the Great North considered that this was an invasion of their territory they prepared to oppose it, but negotiations were started between the two parties with the result that they reached an agreement, and the Great North withdrew their threat of opposition. This agreement included amongst other things the granting of running powers to the Great North over the new line, but for some reason it was never properly completed—for though sealed by the Great North and signed by directors of the Inverness and Nairn the attestation clause was never filled in nor was it dated.

The Great North opposition having been withdrawn, the Inverness and Nairn Bill was duly passed
and the line constructed and opened in November,
1855.

This small beginning did not satisfy Inverness, and
in 1854 a stronger Committee than the Board of the
Inverness and Nairn brought out a proposal for the
continuation of the railway to Elgin, the whole to be
known as the Inverness and Elgin Junction Railway.
Again the Great North objected on the grounds that
if a railway were made from Inverness to Elgin it
would serve the most prosperous part of the country
between Keith and Inverness and as a through connection from Aberdeen was essential they feared that
they would be left to make a railway through the
barren district between Keith and Elgin, which section
also included the expensive crossing of the Spey.
Accordingly as their original powers had by now
elapsed they deposited a Bill to empower them to make
a line from Huntly to Nairn themselves. Negotiations
between the rival parties were entered into and an
agreement was reached on December 5th, 1854, by
which the Inverness people were to make the line to
the Spey from Inverness and the Great North that to
the Spey from Huntly, the crossing to be made at their
joint expense. Mr. Brunel was to be consulted and
to be asked to examine the approaches and crossing
of the Spey "including the heavy works and cuttings
on the East side and the banking and arches on the
West side". He was to decide how the cost should
be equitably divided between the Companies but apparently not the actual site of the crossing. This
point was in dispute and despite further surveys no

THE SPEY VIADUCT.

ELGIN SHED.   Photo: The Locomotive Publishing Co. Ltd.

decision was reached.   Under the terms of the agreement between the parties if an agreement was not
reached in time for the Bills to pass that session they
were both to be withdrawn, except only that part of
the Great North's Bill which gave them powers to
construct their line to Keith, and that is what actually
happened.

In the meantime the Inverness and Elgin Company
had been dissolved and a new one formed which included Lord Fife's Trustees' representatives, the Duke
of Sutherland, Mr. Matheson and others and was
known as the Inverness and Aberdeen Junction Railway.   After the failure of the Bill in 1855 there were
further discussions about where the line was to cross
the Spey, but in the autumn of that year the new Company decided to make the line the whole way from
Nairn to Keith.   They thought, among other things,
that the middle of a river was an inconvenient ending
to their line—as indeed it was,—though apparently
when the original arrangement was come to it was intended that the Great North should work the trains
as far as Elgin and the Inverness Company onwards
from there.

Anyhow, making the line right through to Keith was
a more practical scheme, and this proposal was put to
the Great North directors with the suggestion that
they should subscribe £40,000 towards the building
of the line.   The Inverness Company's Chairman, the
Hon. C. N. Bruce, also undertook in a letter that they
would abide by all the agreements come to in 1854.
The Great North directors thought that they included
the agreement with the Inverness and Nairn Railway

giving them running powers, but this was not in the mind of the Inverness and Aberdeen Junction Railway, whose Chairman some years later told the Parliamentary Committee which was considering their proposal to amalgamate with the Inverness and Perth, that he knew nothing about it. The Great North at that time produced their original of it, which they subsequently lost! As it had never been properly completed it was, of course, not legally binding, and this may be why Mr. Bruce was not told about it, but however that may be, it seems curious that the Great North directors should not have made certain of the inclusion of an agreement which was of such great importance to them. The whole episode is rather mysterious for though this agreement was constantly referred to in the Parliamentary battles which were waged between the two companies during the next forty years, it was never satisfactorily cleared up.

An agreement was eventually reached on Oct. 20th, 1855, for the Inverness and Aberdeen Junction Company to take their line to Keith on condition that the Great North had two directors on the Board in virtue of their subscribing £40,000 towards the cost of constructing the line. Clauses were also inserted in the proposed Bill giving the two Companies powers to give reciprocal running powers and through working agreements. It was stipulated that the money was not to be paid until a certificate was produced by the engineers that there was no gradient steeper than 1 in 60 on the line or any curve sharper than half a mile radius. Nor was the money to be paid till the engineers certified that work costing double the amount the

Great North were to provide had been carried out between Keith and Elgin, including the Spey viaduct. Aberdeen was suspicious that even now Inverness would only make the line as far as Elgin !

As the result of this agreement a Bill was duly deposited and passed in the session of 1856. Work was commenced at once and the line opened for traffic in 1858, thus at last completing the through route from Aberdeen to Inverness as the Great North's line from Huntly to Keith had been open since October 11th, 1856.

At this time the Great North's energies seem to have been mostly devoted to encouraging the construction of branches in Aberdeenshire. They were finding no difficulty in raising money for that purpose, but it seems extraordinary that they should have allowed some one else to make the line for the construction of which they had originally obtained powers, and which was so important to them. Probably local concerns were of greater interest to them and as in the early days the relationships between the two companies were cordial and their interests more or less the same the arrangement seemed satisfactory enough. It was only later when relationships became strained—as they so soon did—and when interests became divergent that the importance of maintaining control of the Northern end was fully realised.

CHAPTER TWO.

THE NORTHERN BRANCHES.

THE credit for being the first railway north of
Aberdeen belongs not to the Great North of
Scotland or the Inverness and Nairn, but the tiny
Morayshire Railway. The idea of a railway to connect
Elgin with Lossiemouth was first suggested in
1841 but the scheme failed from lack of support.
That it was ultimately constructed was due to the
energy and enthusiasm of one man—Mr. James Grant
a banker in Elgin, who was later Provost of that
city and who with his brother started the famous Glengrant Distillery. So convinced was he of the possibilities financial and otherwise of linking Lossiemouth
with Elgin and the Valley of the Spey by rail that he
employed engineers to make surveys and produced
estimates of probable traffics entirely at his own expense. Early in 1844 he convinced the directors of
the Lossiemouth and Stotfield Harbour Company of
the practicality of his scheme and after they had made
a further long and careful survey of their own they
decided to give it their cordial support. Accordingly
on March 3rd, 1845, a meeting of various local interests was held at which there was appointed an acting
Committee to superintend the further progress of the
railway, and a prospectus was issued for a line from
Lossiemouth to Craigellachie to be called the Moray-

shire Railway. The promoters of this scheme did not propose to build the whole line themselves but only the sections Lossiemouth-Elgin and Orton-Craigell-achie as it was intended to use the projected line of the Great North of Scotland between Elgin and Orton. The Capital of the Company was to be £50,000 and applications for over four times that amount were received in little over a month from the time the prospectus was issued. Later there was a suggestion to continue the line to Aberlour and that it should be double throughout—the extra cost of these alterations being estimated at £10,000, and this sum was to be raised by new stock to be allocated among the shareholders. A Bill was deposited in the session of 1846 which, more lucky than many a larger local undertaking, passed all its stages and received the Royal Assent on July 10th of that year. So the Morayshire Railway—"the brave little Bantam that crow'd over all"—started on its career.

The financial crash which hit the Great North so hard was no respecter of persons but affected large and small alike and the Morayshire suffered from it along with the rest. The first General meeting of the Company was held on September 9th, 1846, when the Directors reported that owing to the postponement of the construction of the Great North of Scotland Railway they also proposed to postpone the construction of their line, but they thought that the Elgin-Lossiemouth section might be commenced in the following spring, and this was approved. At a subsequent meeting of the directors Mr. Forteith of Newton was appointed Chairman of the Company.

D

It was not, however, till 1851 that any further progress was made. At a meeting of shareholders on May 28th of that year it was decided to make application to the Commissioners of Railways for leave to abandon the Orton-Craigellachie section of the line as this was dependent on the construction of the Great North line of which there were no signs. The application was granted and leave was given to the Company to reduce their capital to £29,700 of 2,970 shares of £10 each.

It was then decided to go ahead with the Lossie-mouth-Elgin section. The directors were determined to get their line constructed as cheaply as possible and after some search they got in touch with Mr. Samuel, formerly the engineer of the Eastern Counties Railway, who would do what they required. He was appointed their engineer and the railway was constructed to his plans and specifications, and he also designed the first locomotives. So successful were their efforts after economy that including all costs of promotion, etc., the cost per mile was only £4,920— a remarkable figure even allowing for the fact that engineering works were light.

The first sod was cut on Saturday, 30th November, 1851, by Mrs. Grant, the wife of the man who may be described as the father of the Morayshire Railway, to the cheers of the crowd and the firing of cannon. The work was pushed on vigorously though some labour trouble was experienced as the English navvies who were employed objected to the presence on the job of Irishmen. This, however, does not seem to have

OPENING OF THE MORAYSHIRE RAILWAY.—THE TERMINUS AT LOSSIEMOUTH.

By courtesy of "The Illustrated London News."

caused any serious delay and the Railway was duly opened on August 10th, 1852.

The opening was performed with great ceremony. Processions were formed in the Market Square of Elgin and marched to the station for the departure of the first train.   This was timed for 10 a.m. but it was 11 before it got off carrying the directors of the Railway and the Town Council of Elgin.   Many people walked to Lossiemouth and got there in time to see it arrive.   There the day was spent in games and sports. In the evening a dinner was given to seventy guests in Elgin.   This was supposed to start at five o'clock but did not do so till six, owing to the fact that many of the guests had great difficulty in getting back by train so great was the crowd which wished to travel. Trains ran till midnight, and three thousand people were carried by them on the first day with no accident of any sort.

The locomotive stock of the Morayshire consisted at first of two small 2-2-0 tank engines built to a patent design of Mr. Samuel.   They weighed about 14 tons in working order and had 10 by 16 in. cylinders and were built by Neilson & Co. of Glasgow.   The sum charged to their capital account for these two engines was £2,622 7s. 8½d.   Surely a very meticulously accurate entry !   The passenger stock was built by Marshall & Co. of Birmingham and was of the same type as that used on the Woolwich Branch of the Eastern Counties Railway.

It was not for some years after this that the inland part of the original Morayshire plan was achieved. As has already been described the Inverness and Aberdeen Junction Railway obtained powers in 1856 to make the line from Nairn to Keith and this revived the Morayshire's idea of a rail connection between Elgin and the inland parts of the country. Arrangements were accordingly made with the I. & A.J.R. to use their line between Elgin and Orton and powers were obtained to construct a line from there to Rothes and Craigellachie—the Craigellachie station to be situated on the northwest side of the River Spey at the point where Dandaleith station now stands. The line from Orton to Rothes was opened on August 23rd, 1858, and to Craigellachie on December 23rd of the same year.

At first the Morayshire ran its own trains over the I. & A.J. but this arrangement only lasted six weeks—owing, it has been said, to the insufficiency of their locomotive stock. As there were only the two original engines till June 1859 this is not surprising. There was also another difficulty in the way of running through trains—the junction at Elgin with the I. & A.J. was a reverse one so that the engine bringing in a train from Lossiemouth had to get round to the other end of it before it could continue its journey to Orton. After the failure of this arrangement the Morayshire attached its coaches to the I. & A.J. trains between Elgin and Orton and then worked them on to Craigellachie themselves.

A serious dispute, however, arose between the two Companies. The Morayshire claimed the right to handle the traffic between their stations and intermediate stations on the I. & A.J., paying to that Company only a proportion of the rates and fares sufficient

Glen Grant, Morayshire Railway

G.N. of S.R. Locomotive No. 32, Class "Y."

to cover charges for the use of the track and haulage. The I. & A.J. on the other hand contended that these proportions only applied to traffic from one part of the Morayshire system to the other, and that they should have the handling of traffic between their own stations and those of the Morayshire.   The dispute came to a head when they seized the goods at the junctions and the Morayshire then determined to get a through route of their own to the Spey through the Glen of Rothes.   They got powers to do this in 1861 and the line was opened from Elgin to Rothes, where it joined their old line, on January 1st, 1862.

The new line was nine and a quarter miles long and very steeply graded.   Leaving Elgin there is an un- broken climb of about six miles including one and a half miles as steep as 1 in 50, and not much more than a mile of this bank is at an easier grade than 1 in 70. From the summit the line falls all the way to Rothes, including about one and a quarter miles at 1 in 50.

Two more locomotives had in the meantime been supplied by Neilson & Co., one in June 1859 and the other in February 1861.   They were 2-4-0 engines and were called "Glen Grant" and "Lesmurdie".

In the meantime developments had been taking place further south.   To provide an outlet for the Strathspey distilleries which were not served by the I. & A.J. Railway, the Keith and Dufftown Railway was promoted, and an Act was obtained in 1857 to build a line eight and a half miles long between these two places.   The share capital was to be £50,000 with powers to borrow £16,666, and the Great North were empowered to subscribe the sum of £10,000 towards

the cost of construction with the consent of three-
fifths of its shareholders. The line was opened on
February 1st, 1862.

Yet another small Company called the Strathspey
Railway continued this line down to the River Spey
at a point opposite the Morayshire's Craigellachie Station and on up the valley to Abernethy—a total distance of thirty-two and a half miles..   Like all
the rest this line, though nominally independent,
was really promoted by the Great North.   To
judge by the prospectus Strathspey must have been
looked on as a sort of railway El Dorado producing
rich traffics of timber, iron and whiskey !   But there
is reason to think that the construction of this line may
have been prompted by reasons of strategy as well.
By the time it was proposed the Great North's relations with both its neighbours—the Inverness and
Aberdeen Junction and the Scottish North Eastern
Railways—was far from cordial.   By constructing a
line to connect with the Morayshire at Craigellachie
they got a route to Elgin independent of the former
and by its continuation up Speyside to the proposed
Junction with the Inverness and Perth Junction Railway they got an outlet for their traffic independent
of the latter.   It may also have been hoped that it
would take traffic from the Inverness and Perth's
line from Aviemore to Forres, the construction of
which was naturally very unpopular with the Great
North.

The line from Dufftown to Abernethy was opened
on July 1st, 1863. Whatever may have been the
reasons for its construction, it was not a financial

success. By the time that it reached the Highland
line it cost between £300,000 and £400,000, most of
which was produced by the Great North, to whom for
years it proved to be a liability and not an asset.

The Keith & Dufftown and Strathspey Railways
provided between them what is unquestionably the
most picturesque part of the Great North's first line
to Elgin—that part which lies between Auchindachy
and Craigellachie. Though not quite so steeply
graded as the Rothes-Elgin line the Keith to
Craigellachie section is difficult enough for southbound trains. From Craigellachie the line follows
the beautiful Valley of the Fiddich to Dufftown where it crosses it and this is a section of steep
gradients and sharp curves. From Dufftown the rise
continues at the even steeper grade of 1 in 60 for a
further mile and a half till the summit is reached at
the picturesque Loch of Park. From there there is
an almost unbroken fall to Keith, but for much the
greater part of the way at easy gradients.

With a view to effecting a junction with these lines
to the South, the Morayshire got powers to continue
their line across the Spey to join the Strathspey line
when they got their Act permitting them to build their
Elgin-Rothes line. The work on this section, however, was retarded so that its opening might synchron-
ise with the opening of the Strathspey, and it was
accordingly also opened on July 1st, 1863. The name
of the old Craigellachie station was then changed to
Dandaleith—the name Craigellachie being given to
the new Junction Station. After the opening of this
link the Morayshire was worked by the Great North,

who thus at last got a through route to Elgin. They
then took over the Morayshire rolling stock. The two
original Morayshire engines were not taken over, but
Nos. 3 and 4 were, becoming Nos. 41 and 42 in the
Great North lists. They continued to work for many
years—No. 42 being broken up in July 1883 and
No. 41 in January 1885.

The Orton-Rothes Line had been worked by the
Morayshire since the opening of the Elgin-Rothes section, but it was suddenly closed by the Great North in
1866 on the ground that it was no longer necessary.
It was, however, left intact and the rails were not actually taken up until 1907 by when, of course, it had
become entirely overgrown and derelict. The Great
North continued to work the rest of the Morayshire
system till the two Companies were amalgamated in
1881.

The last addition to the Great North system of railways in this part of the world was the extension of the
Speyside line from Abernethy to a junction with the
Highland line near Broomhill, running powers being
exercised over that Company's line for three miles
from Boat of Garten. It had originally been intended
to cross the Spey at Grantown and join the Highland line there, but this idea was abandoned in
favour of this new scheme. To save making a Junction at Broomhill the Highland laid a separate line
alongside their own, traffic being interchanged at Boat
of Garten. The line was opened on August 1st,
1866, and this arrangement has remained in force ever
since.

One other small railway was worked independently for a short time—the Banff, Portsoy and Strathisla Railway, which connected the county town of Banff and the harbour of Portsoy with the important agricultural town of Keith. Its Act of Incorporation was obtained in 1857, by which it was given powers to construct a railway from a junction with the Great North of Scotland at Grange (where there was to be a joint station) to Banff with a branch from Tillynaught to Portsoy. The line was opened on August 2nd, 1859.

As with all the other railways in this part of the country finance was a serious matter for the Banff, Portsoy and Strathisla Railway and its line had to be constructed cheaply, and this, of course, meant severe gradients. From Grange to the summit of Glenbarry is a four mile bank, much of which is at 1 in 100 or worse, and from there to Portsoy on the coast there is an even steeper fall. The first three and a half miles down to Cornhill are almost entirely at a gradient of 1 in 70, and though the gradients are easier from there through Tillynaught Junction, there is a final fall of two miles right into Portsoy Station, of which the first is at 1 in 70 and the last mostly at 1 in 86. This is a very severe bank for southbound trains, and its difficulty is increased by the fact that trains have to start on the very sharp curve on which Portsoy Station is built.

From the opening of the line till the construction of the Coast Line from Portsoy to Elgin, the line from Keith to Banff was the main line and the Tillynaught-Portsoy section was treated as a branch. There was originally a continuation of this branch down to the harbour at Portsoy. Though the metals were not lifted till 1910 the line had not been used for many years previously and was probably closed soon after the opening of the Coast line—an event which no doubt considerably diminished the traffic at Portsoy Harbour; which had been considerable at one time. It is said that the Company bought their engine No. 3 specially for this traffic. The passenger station at Portsoy prior to the opening of the Elgin line was what is now the goods station.

By an Act of 1863 powers were obtained to construct a line along the coast from Portsoy to Portgordon, but they were not used for reasons which will appear later. By the same Act the name of the Company was changed to the Banffshire Railway. From this year it was worked by the Great North of Scotland who then took over its rolling stock. It was finally amalgamated with that Company on August 1st, 1867.

At the time it was taken over the Banffshire's rolling stock consisted of 4 locomotives, 3 first and third class composite coaches, 4 third class coaches, 3 passenger vans, 3 cattle trucks, 63 open wagons and one goods brake van. The first two locomotives were built by Hawthorns of Leith for the opening of the line and were 0-4-2 tanks, having 5 ft. 0 in. or 5 ft. 2 in. coupled wheels and 3 ft. 0 in. trailing wheels. They were said to have been called "Banff" and "Portsoy". No. 3 was an outside cylinder 0-4-2 tender engine which was bought secondhand from the Scottish Central Railway in 1860. It had been built by the Vulcan Foundry, Warrington, for that Railway, in whose

books it was numbered 23, and by whom it was rebuilt before being sold to the Banff, Portsoy and
Strathisla Railway. It is said to have been named
by them "Strathisla". No. 4 was another 0-4-2 outside
cylinder tender engine by Hawthorns, Leith. When
taken over by the Great North these engines received
the numbers 37, 38, 39 and 40. The last was
sold to the Deeside Railway early in 1864 and
when that Company's stock was taken over by
the Great North it resumed its old number in

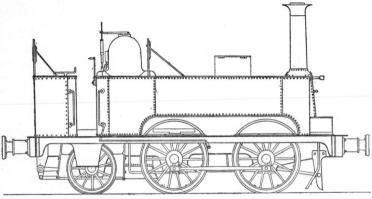

BANFFSHIRE RAILWAY 0-4-2 TANK ENGINE

their books till August 1878, when it was re-
numbered 63. It was scrapped in December 1879.
No. 3 was broken up early in 1868, but Nos. 1 and 2
had a long life on the Great North. One worked on
the Tillynaught and Portsoy branch until it became
part of the coast line, and they are said to have been
used for a time as ballast engines on that line when
it was being built. Both were broken up in January
1885.

While Morayshire and Banffshire were thus being
provided with a railway system, Aberdeenshire was

not being idle in that matter. The first proposals for Branches were the Great North of Scotland (Eastern Extension) and Great North of Scotland (Western Extension) railways which were proposed in 1846. The former would have served the North-eastern part of the county and the latter the district between Inverurie and Banff. It would really have been a sort of combination of the existing Old Meldrum and Macduff lines but would have approached Macduff from the East by a gradient of 1 in 30 and proceeded past the harbour and round the Coast to Banff. Here it would have formed a junction with the branch then proposed by the Great North from Grange to Banff practically where the present Banff Harbour station stands. But these schemes came to nothing and some ten years later a series of Branches off the main Great North line were built which between them brought most of the principal places in the county on to the railway. They were all built by nominally independent Companies, but the Great North helped to finance them and worked them all under contract from the start.

The first of these Branches to be made was the Inverurie and Old Meldrum Junction Railway which was opened on July 1st, 1856. This was a very small affair, branching off from the main line one and a quarter miles north of the then Inverurie Station and having a length of four and three-quarter miles. To avoid a junction at the point where it turned off a line was laid alongside the Great North from Inverurie Station. There was one intermediate station—Lethenty. The Great North were authorised to subscribe to it and to take part in

For the benefit of new r
explained that the interest of
largely upon the readers them
Magazine for the L.N.E.R.
L.N.E.R. staff.

The Magazine costs more
covered by the revenue from
ments, and it is, therefore, no
payment for contributions, no
does the space available make
tee the publication of all
Readers may, however, rest
article or items sent in recei
sideration, and that every e
provide the best selection of
and photographs to suit all g
the company's staff.

Contributions for the nex

its management. As a matter of fact they agreed to work it at prime cost and also gave a guarantee that they would hand over to the new Company half the net receipts accruing to them from their line. They also subscribed £2,000 towards the cost of construction.

The next branch to be opened was that from Inveramsay to Turriff. This was built by a Company known as the Banff, Macduff and Turriff Junction Railway, which had its origin at a meeting held at Pitcaple on October 23rd, 1854. Like the other branches it was nominally independent with Great North representatives on its board its chairman being Mr. Blaikie, who had been the Great North's first chairman. As in the case of the Old Meldrum Line the Great North also gave the new Company a guarantee that they would allow to its shareholders half of the net receipts accruing to them from the traffic of the new Line and they subscribed £40,000 towards the cost of construction. The Act of Incorporation under which powers were obtained to construct the railway from Inveramsay to Turriff received the Royal Assent on June 15th, 1855.

There seems to have been difficulty in getting labour and it is recorded that in the spring of 1857 the navvies working in the South Haddo cutting who were receiving 17/- to 18/- a week were offered an increase to 20/- if they completed that work by July 15th of that year. Whether they succeeded in doing so does not appear, but the line was opened as far as Turriff on September 5th, 1857.

At first a daily train service of 3 passenger and one
goods each way was provided, but in the summer of
1858 this was increased to four passenger trains each
way.   But the line was not a great success financially,
and in the autumn of that year the service was reduced to three mixed trains each way daily.   Even
this did not put matters right as the results of the
working of the year 1859 showed a loss with a worse
one in the following year.   It was estimated that for
the year ending August 31st, 1861, the receipts per
mile per week were only eight pounds.

By this time the line had been continued for a
further eleven and a half miles to Gellymill, known
as Banff and Macduff, about three-quarters of a
mile short of the present terminus at Macduff.
This extension had been carried out by yet another
Company—the Banff, Macduff and Turriff Extension
Railway, and was opened on June 4th, 1860.   The
original Banff, Macduff and Turriff Junction had
by now changed its title to the Aberdeen and Turriff.
There had been a good deal of difficulty in getting
enough money raised locally for this extension and
it was at first intended to go only to Myrehouse, two
miles short of Banff Bridge.   However, money was
then raised to carry the line a mile further and by a
change in the plan for the station here which allowed
the level of the line to be raised, economies were effected which enabled the line to be carried on yet another
three-quarters of a mile.   This alteration in the levels,
however, prevented the construction of a tramway
from the terminus to Macduff Harbour which had
originally been contemplated, but in the altered circumstances the gradient would have been too steep.

The train service provided was entirely mixed, the time taken for the twenty-nine and a half miles varying from ninety-three minutes to two hours! Special provision was made for fishwives to whom third class return tickets at single fare were to be issued at Banff and Macduff to all stations on the Turiff and Macduff line, except Wartle, and also to Inverurie, Kintore, Aberdeen or Insch.   One loaded creel was allowed to each fishwife free of charge, "any additional package to be charged at Scale Rates."

Powers to build the two branches nearest to Aberdeen were not obtained without a considerable Parliamentary battle.   In the year 1856 Bills were promoted by the Alford Valley Railway Company to make a line from Kintore, through Kenmay, Monymusk and Tillyfourie to Alford, and by the Formartine and Buchan Railway to make a line from a junction with the Great North at Dyce to Peterhead and Strichen. These two branches were designed to serve some of the most fertile and prosperous parts of Aberdeenshire.   The Vale of Alford is famous as an agricultural district and from here come some of the best cattle bred in Scotland.   The Buchan district also contains some of the finest agricultural land in Scotland, while on its East and North coasts respectively are situated Peterhead and Fraserburgh, two of the largest towns of Aberdeenshire.   The district, however, was not an easy one in which to make a railway, as going from South to North it had to cross from one river valley to the other, first from the Don to Ythan and then, though more easily, from the Ythan to the Ugie.   This sort of country obviously makes for steep gradients and the Buchan line as finally completed necessarily suffered from this disadvantage.

Both these companies were backed by the Great North and both were opposed by rivals, and only the Alford Valley got through Parliament in that Session.

The first project for a railway to Alford had been that proposed in 1846, but this lapsed and nothing was done for some years.   In 1855 there was a plan to make a railway from a junction with the Great North main line at Buchanstone to Alford, across, or rather through the Bryndie Hill.   This would have involved a tunnel of some 700 yards in length and very severe gradients.   The plan was dropped when it was realised that a line with comparatively good gradients and no tunnel could be made from Kintore through Tillyfourie and this was the line for which Parliamentary sanction was sought.

At about the same time as this plan was proposed another railway to Alford was also suggested.   This idea was to continue the Deeside Railway from Banchory, which was then its terminus, up to Lumphanan and thence by way of Cushnie to Alford.   This line was surveyed but the scheme was dropped in favour of another also promoted by the Deeside Company, which was known as the Deeside and Alford Valley Extension Railway.   It was now proposed that a railway should be made from Colford on the Deeside line and about eight and a half miles from Aberdeen by way of Echt and Waterton to Tillyfourie, whence it would have followed the same route to Alford as that of the Alford Valley.   Both the proposed lines were to have their terminus at a point near the cross-roads which are South of the Bridge of Alford and about one mile from the village itself. The Deeside Extension, however, also proposed a continuance up to Bridgetown.

Both these proposals were put to a meeting at Alford and the Deeside scheme was approved by a very large majority. Parliament, however, thought otherwise. Though the Deeside line served a larger area it was pointed out that a railway having a junction with the Great North of Scotland at Kintore would in effect take the people from the Alford Valley far more easily to the other parts of Aberdeenshire to which they wanted to go than a line which had its terminus in Aberdeen and that at some distance from the Great North. Moreover, it was shorter. The Bill of the Alford Valley Company was, therefore, passed and the line was duly constructed, though to a terminus in the village of Alford and not at the crossroads, as proposed in the Bill. The total length of this line was fifteen miles and the Great North of Scotland subscribed £15,000 towards its construction. It was finally opened on March 21st, 1859.

The Northern area of Aberdeenshire was not so lucky. As has already been mentioned, in 1846 a line known as the Great North of Scotland (Eastern Extension) had been proposed to serve this part of the country but nothing came of it. Again in 1854 there had been a proposal for a railway from Aberdeen to Peterhead, leaving the Great North at Kittybrewster and going straight up from there nearly to Ellon, and thence on much the same course as proposed in the

E

following year for the Formartine and Buchan, but this again fell through. The promoters of the Formartine and Buchan originally only proposed to build a line from a junction with the Great North at Dyce to Auchnagatt—a distance of twenty-one miles—as it was not considered that the financial position would be strong enough to enable it to go further. However, it was subsequently decided to extend it by way of New Maud to Peterhead with a branch to Strichen by way of the west side of the Mormond Hill, and a Bill to obtain powers to do this was deposited in 1856. A rival scheme, known as the Aberdeen, Peterhead and Fraserburgh Railway, had already appeared and likewise deposited a Bill in the same Session. This was generally referred to as Mr. Duncan's line as it was chiefly instigated by him. As Chairman of the Deeside Railway he was also largely at the back of the Deeside and Alford Valley Scheme, and so was at the time attacking the Great North on two fronts This line to Peterhead and Fraserburgh would have had its own station at Aberdeen near Princes Street with a short branch leading down to the harbour. From Aberdeen it would have proceeded due North and, crossing the Don by a bridge thirty feet high, having one arch of two hundred feet span and four of forty-five feet span, followed the coast to Newburgh. There it turned inland by the valley of the Ythan to Ellon and thence proceeded by way of Auchnagatt, Stuartfield and Old Deer to Mintlaw. Here it forked, one line going down by Longside to Peterhead and the other northwards through New Leeds to Fraserburgh. The total distance to Peterhead by this route would have been just over forty-two miles and to Fraserburgh just short of forty-five miles. It was unpopular in Aberdeen as it went right through the links—a favourite playground—and suffered from the serious disadvantage of having no physical connection with the other railways except by the lines along the harbour.

Mr. Duncan was at first successful, for the committee of the House of Commons found the preamble of his Bill proved. It failed, however, to comply with the Standing Order of the House of Lords, and was therefore lost, so Buchan got no railway that year.

In the following year both companies produced new Bills, but both were thrown out through failure to comply with the Standing Orders.

In order to try and get all the support they could the Formartine and Buchan had a fresh survey made in 1857 and their Bill of 1858 proposed that their line should fork at Mintlaw and follow much the same course as had been proposed by their rivals. As the line passed to the west of Ellon there was also to be a branch to serve that town. Powers were also sought to double the Great North line from Dyce to Kittybrewster.

The case for the Formartine and Buchan was that by taking the inland route for the first part of its course it would serve a wider area than a line along the coast and by its junction with the Great North it would make a better link between the northern parts of Aberdeenshire and the rest of the county than a line having no physical connection with any other railway. Moreover, by its route round by New Deer it would serve the local requirements better than its rival going by Stuartfield. These arguments seem to have impressed the Parliamentary Committee which considered the rival schemes, and they reversed the decision come to in 1856 and the Buchan and Formartine was passed and Mr. Duncan's rejected.

The prolonged Parliamentary Battle seems to have killed the local interest in the line and there was great difficulty in raising enough money locally for its construction.   The Great North having spent £25,000 on this contest were very anxious to get the line built and were very active in its support.   But money from its extremities was not forthcoming so it was decided to begin by making the line only as far as Mintlaw, where the Fraserburgh branch was planned to leave it.   A short Act was obtained in 1859 allowing an alteration in the route by which the line was brought to within half a mile of Ellon and the branch previously proposed to serve that town was abandoned. The line was opened to Mintlaw on July 18th, 1861, and reached Peterhead—money now being forthcoming—on July 3rd, 1862.   Fraserburgh, however, still had to wait for some time before getting its railway. By an Act passed in 1863 the proposed line from Mintlaw was abandoned and the original scheme of the Formartine and Buchan of a line from Maud by way of Strichen and Lonmay was authorised.   It was opened on April 24th, 1865.   The whole of the Formartine and Buchan was, of course, worked by the Great North from the first, and they subscribed £50,000 to tbe cost of making it.

CHAPTER THREE.

THE DEESIDE RAILWAY.

THE Deeside Railway, like the Morayshire and Banffshire Railways, was built and worked for some time by an independent Company. The first meeting of its promoters was held in Aberdeen on September 2nd, 1845, when the joint committees of the Aberdeen and Great North of Scotland Railways decided to build a line at least as far as Banchory. Plans were prepared and a prospectus was issued from which we learn that the original capital was to consist of 2,000 shares of £50 each and the provisional Committee was to be composed of the directors of the Aberdeen and Great North of Scotland Railways, under the chairmanship of Lord Provost Thomas Blaikie. A suggestion was made that the South Deeside turnpike should be used for the railway but this scheme was rejected on the advice of the engineer, who strongly favoured a route along the North bank of the river. The line was, of course, to be single, and the estimated cost was £95,009. 19s. 1d. !

The Company's prospects appeared bright and the public were informed that " It was remarked so long ago as the year 1811 by the late Dr. Skene Keith in his statistical account and survey of Aberdeenshire that if the legislature saw the importance of the Forest of Mar in the proper light an Iron Railway might at no distant date be seen on the Banks of the Dee. At that time Locomotives had not been invented and the benefit of Railway Travelling was not known. The case, however, is now widely different. There is a daily mail and stage coach on the line and the Post travelling is better than on any other road in the county. This fact and the great demand for timber, especially Railroad Sleepers, at the present time from the forests along the Banks of the River, has suggested the enquiry whether the traffic would not make a Railroad a profitable investment and on enquiry the result has exceeded all expectations."

It was proposed to improve the Fords and Ferries over the river and to build a new bridge over it nearly opposite Durris House. A moderate estimate of tolls on the North and South Turnpike Roads to Banchory showed an average taking of upwards of £7,000 per annum over a period of five years. About £2,000 a year was also spent on floating timber down the river, traffic which was expected to be diverted to the Railway, and "as it is anticipated by those who know the beautiful scenery and superb climate of Deeside that such a linking of Aberdeen Port and main lines would produce a larger increase of passengers than usual" the estimated receipts were put at £14,000. The expenses were estimated at £5,000 so allowing a profit of £9,000 a year. To save the expenses of rolling stock it was proposed to sell or lease the line to the Aberdeen Railway Company.

It was then proposed to continue the railway to Aboyne by way of Kincardine O'Neil. A survey of the route was made, and at a meeting held on Sept.

29th, 1845, it was decided to construct the whole line to
Aboyne and to increase the capital of the company to
£220,000.   Westwards from Banchory the line
would have been almost parallel to the main
Deeside road nearly as far as Kincardine O'Neil.
It would have passed to the south of that village
on an embankment and crossed the river about
half a mile to the west, recrossing it again
about a mile further on where it runs from
south to north, and above the Mill of Dess. Further
west it would have made a sweep round by the north
of Aboyne Loch, actually crossing a small part of it,
and finished in Aboyne village north of the main
road and not far from where the East Lodge of Aboyne
Castle now stands. The total length of the railway
from its junction with the Aberdeen Railway at Ferryhill to Aboyne would have been twenty-nine and a
quarter miles.

The summit level of the line would have been 447
feet above the sea at a point about a mile east of
Aboyne. The steepest gradient would have been 1 in
103.   The most extensive cutting—at Sluie—would
have been a mile and a half long with a maximum
depth of 40 feet. There would have been two considerable banks, one from Invercannie to Sluie three
miles long at gradients varying from 1 in 103 to 1 in
119, and the other from the second crossing of the
river to the summit of the line—two and a half miles
at 1 in 103. There were no sharp curves and altogether the line would have been a much easier one to
work than the existing one by Torphins.

This scheme was approved by Parliament and the
Act of Incorporation of the Deeside Railway received

the Royal Assent on July 6th, 1846. It was, however, never carried out for at a meeting held on Sept. 4th, following, it was decided to postpone construction for a year until the Aberdeen line was more nearly completed, as the work could be carried out more cheaply by the plant of that railway than by a separate plant.

As in the case of the Great North of Scotland financial difficulties now arose which prevented anything more being done. This state of affairs continued for the next few years and in 1848 some shareholders petitioned for a dissolution of the Company and a division of its assets. This was prevented, but shortly after this the whole of the Company's shares passed into the possession of the Aberdeen Railway Company. The Deeside had previously lent the amounts paid up on their shares to the Aberdeen Company who now repaid these sums to the shareholders, taking the shares in exchange. In 1849 other people began to take an interest in the construction of a railway up Deeside and the whole of the old shares were re-sold to them by the Aberdeen Company.

Matters now began to move. Mr. Duncan had become the Chairman and Mr. Davidson of Inchmarlo, the Deputy Chairman, and it was thanks mainly to their efforts that the line was built. In 1850 a committee was appointed to make terms with the landowners through whose property the Railway was to pass, and they mostly proved willing to let the Company have the land on favourable terms. There were some further delays but at the General Meeting on Nov. 25th, 1851, the directors recommended that the construction of the railway should be undertaken to

Banchory on a new survey made by Messrs. Locke
and Errington, and the contractors had undertaken
to make the line for £65,000. A Bill was deposited
for the session of 1852 by which the capital of the
Company was reorganised, the time for constructing
the line to Banchory was extended, the new plan was
approved, and the line from Banchory to Aboyne was
abandoned. This Act was passed in that session and
so what was in fact a new Company started to construct the Deeside Railway. The first sod of the new
line was cut by Mrs. Kinloch of Park on the lands of
Park on July 5th, 1852, and the works were pushed on
so fast that the railway was opened for traffic on
September 8th, 1853.

The Aberdeen Railway had been opened in 1850
with a terminus at Ferryhill and at first the Deeside
used this station. But when the Aberdeen Railway
made their extension to their new Guild Street Station, the Deeside went with them and used their
station from its opening on August 2nd, 1854, till the
Denburn line was completed. For the use of the Guild
Street Station the Deeside paid £700 a year for the
first three years and £1,000 a year after that, with
provisions for a further rise if and when their traffics
exceeded £12,000 a year.

The Deeside line itself had five stations, namely,
Cults, Murtle, Culter, Park, Mills of Drum and Banchory. A private platform was built at Crathes in
1853 for the use of Crathes Castle. This was closed
and a public station erected in 1863 when that at Mills
of Drum was closed.

The original train service consisted of three passenger trains in each direction as follows :

				a.m.	a.m.	p.m.
—	Aberdeen	depart	...	7.0	11.0	4.30
3¼	Cults	,,	...	7.12	11.12	4.42
4¾	Murtle	,,	...	7.18	11.18	4.48
7	Culter	,,	...	7.26	11.26	4.56
10¼	Park	,,	...	7.38	11.38	5.8
12½	Mills of Drum	,,	...	7.46	11.47	5.17
16¼	Banchory	arrive	...	8.0	12.0	5.30
—	Banchory	depart	...	8.30	12.30	6.30
	Mills of Drum	,,	...	8.44	12.43	6.43
	Park	,,	...	8.53	12.52	6.52
	Culter	,,	...	9.5	1.4	7.4
	Murtle	,,	...	9.13	1.12	7.12
	Cults	,,	...	9.18	1.18	7.18
	Aberdeen	arrive	...	9.30	1.30	7.30

First and third class accommodation only was provided.

It was arranged with Mr. Cook of the Huntly Arms Hotel, Aboyne, that he should provide a coach service between Banchory and Aboyne to connect with the trains at Banchory.

At first the line was worked by the Scottish Central Railway with joint rolling stock of the Scottish Central, Scottish Midland, and Aberdeen Companies, but this arrangement was soon abandoned, and the Deeside railway provided itself with rolling stock of its own.

Financially the line was a success and a dividend of five per cent. was paid from the start.   This no doubt encouraged the promotion of the scheme to make a railway from Banchory to Lumphanan and Alford which, as has been seen, was dropped in favour of the Deeside and Alford line, which would have left the Deeside at Colford. This also came to nothing, being defeated in Parliament by the Alford Valley line of the Great North of Scotland, but while that battle was taking place there was a new demand for the continuation of the Deeside line to Aboyne. A Bill was, therefore, deposited in the session of 1857 for a line from Banchory to Aboyne by way of Torphins and Lumphanan. By taking the line by this route instead of by Kincardine O'Neil as had been originally intended about two miles were added to its length and some very steep gradients were necessitated. Immediately after leaving Banchory Station there is a $2\frac{1}{2}$ mile climb mostly at 1 in 68 and then after a fall of about a mile there is another bank of four and a half miles which though it begins easily enough ends with three and a quarter miles at 1 in 70. This bank ends in a deep cutting known as Satan's Den, and this is the summit of the line. From there to Aboyne is mostly down hill, much of which is as steep as 1 in 70. It was claimed, however, that the engineering works involved would be less costly than those on the shorter route, that more traffic would be forthcoming and that cheap land was available.

The Bill duly passed through Parliament and received the Royal Assent on July 27th, 1857. The first sod of this new line was cut at Rosehall near Aboyne by the Marchioness of Huntly on October 3rd of that year before a large crowd of people. To celebrate the event the Company provided a "plain cold lunch", their share of the expenses of the celebrations being limited to one hundred pounds. Nearly two years were spent in building the line, which was opened to traffic on September 3rd, 1859.

The financial arrangements of the Deeside extension Railway, as the line from Banchory to Aboyne was called, were peculiar. Though it was part of the Deeside Company and built by them advantage was taken of the fact that its shareholders were different people to the original Deeside shareholders to make the two practically independent concerns. Dividends on the new shares were paid only out of the profits of the new line. Two new directors were added to the Board to watch the extension shareholders' interests, but could not vote on the question of the original shareholders' dividends who were also debarred from voting about the extension's dividend. This arrangement was greatly to the advantage of the original shareholders whose dividends had never been less than five per cent. and they increased steadily until they reached eight per cent. in the years 1863-1864 and 1865. The extension shares, however, only paid two per cent. during those years, having paid next to nothing for the first three years.

Two years after the opening of the extension line the Deeside found themselves in the happy position of being of strategic importance to both the other railways serving Aberdeen. As will be seen in the next Chapter the Scottish North Eastern was quarrelling violently with the Great North of Scotland over the question of a joint station in Aberdeen and they were proposing to get a through route of their own to the

North by a line from Stonehaven to Kintore. This
line was to have had a junction with the Deeside line
at Culter by which trains could run from Aberdeen
to the north and the Scottish North Eastern approached the Deeside with a view to getting running
powers over their line from Aberdeen to Culter. But
the terms they offered were not good enough so the
Deeside Chairman offered to lease his Company to the
Great North of Scotland.

This proposal of the Scottish North Eastern
was a serious threat to the Great North as it
would have given the Scottish North Eastern an
alternative route from Aberdeen to the North, and
as the Deeside used their station in Aberdeen a
through route from the South would have been made
available even without the construction of the Stone-
haven-Culter line. The Great North realised this at
once and promptly accepted the Deeside's terms. The
Scottish North Eastern were furious and made further efforts to get the Deeside but without success, but
this effort forced the Great North to take over £30,000
worth of unappropriated Extension shares worth
probably £1,500. Some of the Deeside directors
were also angry, and as the lease had not been approved by Parliament they managed to get an inter-
dict against it which in the following year was made
perpetual. The plan, therefore, miscarried for the
moment, but not for long for in 1866 when the Great
North got powers to amalgamate all the small northern branch line Companies with themselves, they also
got powers to lease the Deeside despite the strong opposition of the Scottish North Eastern.

Under this Act the Deeside Railway was leased to the Great North for a term of 999 years. The latter Company had to pay the original Deeside shareholders a dividend of $7\frac{1}{2}$ per cent. and the Extension shareholders a dividend of three per cent. for the first year and three and a half per cent. thereafter. It was also arranged that if and when the gross revenue of Deeside line and its extension was more than £27,000 in any financial year, half the excess of that amount should go to each Company—the Deeside's half to be equally divided between their two classes of shareholders. A Managing Committee consisting of three directors of each Company was to be appointed to manage the Deeside and in particular they were to fix the number of trains to be run, which in any event was not less than the number run before the lease became valid, and the rates then in force were not to be increased.

So the Great North won its battle and the Deeside was at last leased to it as from Sept. 1st, 1866, but the cost had been high.

While this battle was being waged a further extension up Deeside had been proposed. Aboyne is less than halfway up the valley of the Dee, and though westward from there the country becomes less fertile, and beyond Cambus O'May much narrower, there were valuable forests in upper Deeside and, of course, Balmoral. Further up still is the village of Braemar and the construction of the line to that point was a logical proposition—though in those days the construction of such a line must have been rather an act of faith, for the tourist traffic had hardly begun to

THE KING'S MESSENGER.

CULTER STATION.

Photo: *J. Valentine & Sons.*

develop—even in 1865 there were practically no
through bookings from the Scottish North Eastern to
the Deeside. Nevertheless such a line was proposed
to meet the local requirements. The engineering
works involved were light, except at the very start
where a short tunnel, followed by a long cutting, was
necessary, so cheapness of construction could be set
off against the prospects of light traffic.

This extension was proposed by an independent
Company called the Aboyne and Braemar Railway
Company. A Bill was deposited for the session of
1865 to give them powers to construct a railway between these two places. According to the plans submitted with the Bill it followed the course of the new
Deeside turnpike road pretty closely for most of its
course. At about the 55th mile post on the road it
would have crossed the River Dee and continued
along its South Bank to a point about a quarter of a
mile short of Braemar where the terminal station was
to have been.

Before the Bill came to the Committee of the House
of Commons it had been decided to proceed with the
line only as far as the Bridge of Gairn about a mile
west of Ballater. The terminal station, however, was
to be in Ballater and the line west of that was only to
be used for goods traffic. In this form the Bill was
passed but provisions were inserted in it that no extension of this Railway was to be made without a local
Act of Parliament specially obtained for that purpose
and expressly authorising it. There had been some
talk of extending the railway through the mountains
to a junction with the Highland line at Blair Atholl,

but counsel denied this intention during the Committee stage of the Bill. Another deviation from the original plan was also made between Dinnet and Cambus O'May. Instead of following the new road between those two places it was diverted to the South and now runs practically parallel with the original Deeside Turnpike which was abandoned in 1857.

The Railway was opened to Ballater on Oct. 17th, 1866, but was not fully completed beyond there at that time. In 1868 it was agreed between James Ross Farquharson, the then Laird of Invercauld and Monaltrie and the Aboyne and Braemar, Great North of Scotland and Deeside Railways that he should construct a standard gauge railway or tramway from Ballater to Bridge of Gairn. It was to connect there with a tramway which he was proposing to construct for about twelve miles towards Braemar to carry the wood traffic from the Ballochbuie Forest. Under this agreement the railway was completed to the Gairn and a bridge built across that river. The rails were actually laid but nothing further was done and the line was never used nor was the tramway ever made. It was at about this time that the Ballochbuie Forest was leased by Queen Victoria and it was probably this that made further works unnecessary.

The train service provided at the opening of the Ballater extension consisted of three through trains in each direction between Aberdeen and Ballater, one more to and from Aboyne, and another to and from Banchory. By this time there were fifteen intermediate stations and all trains called at every one of them except the 1.35 p.m. up, which passed six smaller

ones, and did the journey in 2 hours and 5 minutes,
and the 4.0 a.m. down, which was first class only,
called only at Banchory and Aboyne and reached
Ballater at 5.50. The best of the others took 2 hours
13 minutes up and 2 hours 25 minutes down for the
forty-three and a quarter miles. The 4.0 a.m. down
was the "Queen's Messenger" as were two Sunday
trains—one each way—run specially for the convey-
ance of Her Majesty's Messengers with her despatches.

The "Messenger Trains" as they were called were a
unique feature of railway work for many years and
their history is an interesting one. In the early 'sixties
the Queen's despatches were brought by train to Perth
and by road from there to Balmoral over the hills by
Blairgowrie and the Cairnwell. After this had been
going on for several years it occurred to the Deeside
Railway that they might convey the messengers with
advantage to themselves. So in the summer of 1864
the Secretary wrote to General Grey, the Queen's
Private Secretary, and proposed that they should run
special trains between Aberdeen and Aboyne in connection with those to and from London. They undertook to perform the journey from Aberdeen to Balmoral in 3 hours 40 minutes, allowing 15 minutes at
Aboyne for changing from rail to road and a carriage
and pair was to be provided to take the messenger the
last part of the journey. Their charge for this service
was to be £9 2s. 0d. for each day on which the trains
ran. After some correspondence this arrangement
was agreed to and the first Queen's Messenger duly
ran on October 8th, 1865, in connection with the train
which had left London the previous morning. The

F

down train left Aberdeen at 4.0 a.m. and calling only at Banchory reached Aboyne at 5.25.   The return train left Aboyne at 2.15 p.m., and also calling at Banchory arrived at Aberdeen at 3.33 p.m.

With the opening of the railway to Ballater the trains were continued to that station, the 4.0 a.m. running in its old times to Aboyne, Ballater, as has been seen, being reached at 5.50.   Special trains continued to run on Sundays, the up train leaving Ballater at 10.25 a.m. and reaching Aberdeen at 12.5 connecting with the train to the South which left at 12.32, the return train leaving Aberdeen at 12.40 and reaching Ballater at 2.30.   Both called at Banchory and Aboyne only.

The up week-day train was not run at this time and the Messenger presumably was taken by the 1.35 which reached Aberdeen at 3.40.   Two years later, however, there was a train which left Ballater at 2.10 and reached Aberdeen at 4 p.m.   By 1880 the departure of the up train had gone back 5 minutes, but there were complaints from the Railway Company of the late arrival of the Messenger at Ballater with consequent delays to the train.   In the following year its departure time was put back to 3.5 p.m., and the arrival time at Aberdeen became 4.30.   By then there were two down Sunday trains, one at 3.30 a.m., calling at Banchory and Aboyne and reaching Ballater at 5.15, and the other at 1 p.m , which was due at Ballater at 2.50.   In 1882 the down morning train lost its regular stops but would set down passengers from the South at any station and reached Ballater at 5 o'clock—a timing which it retained for the rest of its life.   All these trains were first-class only, though third-class

By courtesy of *L.N.E.R.*

DEESIDE TRAIN IN THE OLD ABERDEEN JOINT STATION.

accommodation was provided for first-class passengers' servants.

By the end of the century third-class passengers were also carried and the up afternoon train had been put back by another hour. In its final form before the War it left Ballater at 4.15 and reached Aberdeen at 5.30, the Messenger going on by a West Coast train which then left Aberdeen at 5.45. The Sunday trains had also been quickened but no attempt was ever made to run them at more than moderate speed.

During the War when the King did not go to Balmoral these trains, of course, did not run, but they were revived in 1919 though not the daily up afternoon train. After that they continued to run regularly till 1937, but in 1938 the old arrangement of sending the Messengers over the hills was restored and the trains were withdrawn. That, however, is going rather beyond the scope of this book.

In the early 'eighties these "Messenger" trains were partly the cause of a law-suit which created a considerable amount of stir at the time. By the Feu Charter granted to the Railway Company for the land on which their station at Crathes was built all passenger trains were bound to stop there. The Messengers, however, did not do so. The Railway Company took the attitude that they were not passenger trains within the meaning of the Act. Moreover, as express trains had not been contemplated at the time of the granting of the Feu Charter they would not admit their obligation to stop any such trains either. They won their case in the Inner House in Edinburgh, but were defeated on appeal to the House of Lords. The case is

remarkable for some very plain speaking by the
Judges in both Courts and under the heading of
" The Law's Uncertainties " an extract from two of
them was published in the "Aberdeen Journal" at the
time which is a good example of Judges differing and
is worth quoting in full.

" THE LAW'S UNCERTAINTIES.

The following verbatim extracts from the judg-
ments delivered recently by Lord Young in the Court
of Session, and Lord Bramwell in the House of Lords,
in the Crathes railway case recently reported, will illus-
trate ' the law's uncertainties ' :—

LORD YOUNG.—The *action* before us is so *ex facie* nimious and un-reasonable as to excite prejudice against it, and one has to be on his guard to see that the exact legal rights of the parties, however un-reasonable, are satisfied . . . . Indeed, the action is altogether so nimious and unreasonable—almost scandalously so—as to start a pre-judice against the pursuer when he makes such a demand. The Judge, indeed, requires to be on his guard against such prejudices to see that the party making such a demand gets the full measure of his rights.

LORD BRAMWELL.—It seems to me that the *defence* before us is so *ex facie* nimious and unreasonable as to excite prejudice against it, and one has to be on his guard to see that the exact legal rights of the parties, however unreason-able, are satisfied . . . I will not say that the defence is a scandalous one, because I have no doubt that it is a *bona fide* one. It is an extravagant one in my opinion, I must say."

This story of the Royal Messenger trains has taken
us far beyond the life of the Deeside Company and
we must now go back to where we left it at the opening of the line from Aboyne to Ballater.   It continued
to work its own trains for about a year after that, but
when the Great North got direct access to it by the
opening of the Denburn line they took over its
working.

The arrangement between the two Companies
worked very well and the railway prospered so that

fresh capital expenditure became necessary for making more crossing places and improving the line. As some difficulty was experienced in deciding how this capital was to be apportioned between them, they decided to amalgamate, and by an Act of Parliament passed in 1876 the Deeside and its Extension were retrospectively amalgamated with the Great North as from August 31st, 1875, and the Aboyne and Braemar as from January 31st, 1876.

It now only remains to describe the rolling stock. When it was decided to work its own trains two tank engines were ordered from Messrs. Hawthorn's of Leith. The first of these was delivered in February 1854, and the second in August of the same year. Another engine, an 0-4-2 tender engine, came from Messrs. Dodds of Rotherham at about the same time. These three did all the work for nearly three years when another engine was supplied by Messrs. Hawthorn's. This was an 0-4-2 tender engine and was numbered 4. With a view to the opening of the Aboyne extension another 0-4-2 came from the same builders in July 1859 and another followed in November of the same year. It appears that these engines were given the numbers 5 and 7, No. 6 being allotted to a similar engine which came in June 1860. Another engine was bought from the Banffshire (or Great North of Scotland) early in 1864. This was Banffshire No. 4 which had been given the Great North number 40 on being taken into their stock in 1863 and which it took again when that Company took over the Deeside engines, but its Deeside number is uncertain. It had to be drawn along the Aberdeen harbour from Waterloo to Guild Street by horses as the Town Council would not allow it to proceed under its own steam, though as a matter of fact it had enough steam in it to help. The Deeside's last engine was another 0-4-2 which came in 1866 and was given a larger tender to allow it to work the Royal Train to Aboyne without stopping at Banchory for water.

The Deeside engines were painted dark blue with black lines and were always kept in magnificent condition. No. 2 tank engine was at one time painted tartan either Royal Stuart or Duff as it was used to work the Queen's Messenger.

When the Great North of Scotland Railway took over the Deeside rolling stock they brought engines Nos. 2, 4, 5, 6, 7 and 8 into their list and gave them the numbers 39 and 49-53 respectively. The ex-Banffshire No. 4 was also taken over and re-numbered 40 as has been told. Deeside tank No. 1 was sold in 1865 as being too light for the traffic, but what became of No. 3 is uncertain. Presumably it was replaced by the Banffshire engine. No. 4 was the first to be scrapped and it went in 1875, No. 5 went in 1876, No. 7 in 1877, No. 6 in 1878 and No. 8 in 1880. Curiously enough No. 2, the oldest of the lot, outlived them all and lasted till July 1883. The ex-Banffshire engine went, as has been seen, in December 1879. Unfortunately these rather scanty details of the old Deeside engines are all that are now available.

DEESIDE RAILWAY, LOCOMOTIVE No. 4.

CHAPTER FOUR.

STRUGGLE.

FOR the first few years of its life the Great North of Scotland was a prosperous railway and paid good dividends, but this happy state of affairs did not last long as it was based on insecure foundations. Moreover, its directors unfortunately possessed a fatal faculty for quarrelling and before many years had passed they were at open war with both their most important neighbours.

Though their relationships with the Inverness and Aberdeen Junction Company had started by being friendly, they soon changed and there were constant rows. The cause of the final rupture seems to have come from the desire of the Inverness and Aberdeen Junction Company to increase their capital by £200,000 and subscribe £15,000 to the Ross-shire Railway. The Great North representatives objected to this on the grounds that so large an increase of capital was unnecessary, as only a short time before £75,000 had been considered sufficient for their purpose, and that this large issue of Preference Stock would depreciate the value of the original shares too far. They proposed that the Great North should buy plant for them, lend them money, and enter into negotiations for a working agreement for carrying on the business of the line. This suggestion raised the wrath of the

Highlanders who refused to consider it, and in 1859 they bought out the Great North by repaying their £40,000 loan on the ground that "they did not work very harmoniously as shareholders." These Highlanders seem to have been very anxious to get rid of the Aberdonians for they bought them out at par, though the £10 shares at that time were only worth about £9-£9 10s. As the latter would at that time get a better return from their own Company, they were probably only too willing to agree to the transaction.

An Act was passed in the following year which formally repealed the loan and the power of the Great North to appoint directors to the Inverness and Aberdeen Junction Board. The clauses in the Act of 1856 enabling the two Companies to make working agreements were, however, re-enacted.

It is probable, however, that there was more in all this than met the eye, for Inverness had never given up its hope that some day it would get more direct railway communication with the South, and possibly the Inverness and Aberdeen Junction people thought that in the event of such a scheme materialising they would have a freer hand if they were entirely independent of the Great North.

To meet the competition of the Aberdeen Steam Navigation Company for the Moray Firth traffic in 1859 the Great North put on a small steamer between Invergordon and Inverness to collect Ross-shire traffic and another between Granton and the Moray Firth, but both these services resulted in loss so were very soon withdrawn.

There was at that time great dissatisfaction

throughout the North with the service provided by the Great North Company and there is no doubt that in those days it was a very bad railway. The lack of any through rail communication from North to South at Aberdeen was a great hardship to the North, and to add to this inconvenience the Great North refused to quote through rates by rail, which greatly annoyed the Inverness and Aberdeen Junction Railway. Moreover, they flatly refused to join the Clearing House, for they were afraid that the share which they would get of the through rates would be small and that would involve them in a heavy loss as their rates were high.

This fear also involved them in another policy which was particularly obnoxious to their neighbours. A great deal of the traffic from the North East of Scotland to London was carried by sea and to get this traffic transferred to themselves the railways interested had drastically reduced their rates. The Great North realised that if they joined this railway league their share of the through rates would be small so they approached the Aberdeen Steam Navigation Company with a suggestion that they should both reduce their rates for through traffic and so keep it in its old channel to the mutual advantage of both, but owing to a difference of opinion as to the proportions of this reduction which each should bear, these negotiations failed. At that time their deputy chairman, Mr. John Stewart, was also a director and principal shareholder of the Steamship Company, but owing to a disagreement with them on matters of policy, he was put off their Board and promptly started a new Company of his own which became known as the

Northern Steam Company. This Company received a small subsidy (£1,500) from the Great North and as their relations with it were very close they naturally wanted to send as much traffic that way as possible and they refused to quote through rates to the South by rail. Incidentally the harbour at Aberdeen was the gainer by this—a fact which probably weighed with an Aberdonian directorate.

This policy was not so obstructive to local trade in those days as it might seem to-day. There were still a great many people who preferred to run the risk of seasickness to the certainty of an uncomfortable journey by rail. A great many people also preferred to send their cattle and goods by sea, as the deliveries were more regular that way than if they went over-land. But it was hardly a policy which would commend itself to the neighbouring railways.

Their treatment of passengers was no better than that of goods. Their trains were very slow and their time-keeping erratic. When the line was opened to Keith the services consisted of five trains in each direc-tion, of which only two were for passengers only, the others being either mixed or goods. The fastest, which was the Mail, left at 3 p.m., and took two hours and forty minutes, while the slowest mixed took three hours and twenty-five minutes. By the early 'sixties the service was not much better. The "Special Passenger and Mail First Class only" which then left at 1.30 p.m., took two hours and thirty-seven minutes to get to Keith, though it did manage to pass five stations without stopping. The up Mail took two hours and forty-five minutes and the other trains from two hours and forty minutes to three hours and five minutes. There is a note in the time table that Gentlemen's Servants accompanying their Masters were booked Third Class by special Mail Trains, but Ordinary, Ordinary return, Excursion, Composition, Scholars and other Periodical Tickets were not available by these trains. One seemed to have to pay a high price for something infinitesimally better than the ordinary when one travelled by one of them! Perhaps the thrill of actually passing a station or two was looked upon by the Company as being worth it, though it is more than doubtful if anyone else can have thought so.

It is true that there were only first and third classes, but third class fares were the equal of most Companies' second—except, of course, by the Parliamentary which was also "mixed" and still managed to fill up no less than three hours and five minutes on its journey of fifty-three miles. For that matter the Inverness and Aberdeen Junction of those days was not much better, and the best through train from Aberdeen to Inverness took five hours and twenty minutes for the journey of 108 miles—oddly enough, this was not the "Special Mail and First Class only" but the ordinary 4.40 p.m. passenger. The best up train was slightly quicker—the special first class and Mail, which left Inverness at 6.40 a.m. and took five hours and a quarter. In one respect the Great North service of those days was ahead of that provided during most of its history—there was one train each way on Sundays described as Passenger, Parliamentary and Mail which ran at the same time as the daily Special First Class and Mail.

Needless to say, the branch services were no better. Kintore to Alford (16½ miles) took an hour.   Aberdeen to Old Deer and Mintlaw (35½ miles), which was as far as the Buchan line had then got, took two hours, while the little "Banffshire" managed to fill up an hour on the sixteen miles between Grange and Banff. And there were not many trains either—five each way a day between Aberdeen and Keith, with three or four on the branches, was considered sufficient for the needs of those days.

A bad train service was not the only thing which troubled passengers on the Great North in the early 'sixties for they were treated in a most high-handed way.   There were very rigid rules about the punctual departure of trains and those passengers who were not in good time were treated rather like malefactors. No doubt on a single line it is particularly desirable that trains should run punctually in order to avoid delays to other trains at crossing places, but the Great North carried it altogether too far.   Once the stationmaster had given the signal to go the guard immediately started his train, even if there was an intending passenger only a few yards off.   Despite all this, punctuality was not an outstanding characteristic of the Railway.

The rigid enforcement of these rules was particularly irksome at Aberdeen.   Communication between the two stations was made by 'buses which were run by the railway and the charge for their use was included in the through fare.   In these circumstances passengers not unnaturally thought that the railway was bound to keep the connection for them.   Only

three-quarters of an hour was allowed between the
arrival of the train from the South and the departure
of the one to the North, and passengers who wanted
to make the connection had to hustle considerably—
even when the South train was punctual, which it frequently was not—or they would find themselves
locked out with the choice of waiting three hours or
taking a special—the latter being what the railway
hoped they would do.

It is said that on one occasion a director who was
thus locked out smashed the window and so got in.
On another occasion a well-known M.P. had the morti-
fication of seeing his family and luggage sent on while
he himself was left behind—an episode of which he
reminded the General Manager some years later when
he was serving on a Parliamentary Committee dealing
with one of the Company's Bills.   According to
another story a party of influential Highlanders who
were locked out and had to spend the night in Aberdeen instead of Inverness were so furious that they
decided then and there to build a line of their own and
so be free of the iniquities of Aberdeen.   Whether this
is historically accurate or not there is little doubt but
that the high-handed behaviour of the Great North
authorities hastened the building of that line. Seldom
can iniquity have brought a more speedy or condign
penalty !

The blow fell in 1861 when a Company known as
the Inverness and Perth Junction Railway obtained
powers to build a line from a junction with the Inverness and Aberdeen Junction at Forres to an end
on junction at Birnam with the already exist-

ing line from that place to Perth and which
was amalgamated with it. This line was opened
for traffic in 1863 and thus the desire for a short
route from Inverness to the South was gratified.
The Company working the new line was virtually
the same as the Inverness and Aberdeen Junction
who owned the lines North of Inverness as
well as those between Inverness and Keith and they
put as much traffic on it as possible, even refusing to
quote through rates or issue through tickets by
Aberdeen.

Two years after the Inverness and Perth line was
opened it was amalgamated with the Inverness and
Aberdeen Junction under the title of the Highland
Railway. The relations between those Companies and
the Great North were now very strained and in addition to quarrels over through bookings there were dis-
putes about the timing of trains. The Great North
realised that once the amalgamation was effected they
would be completely side-tracked as far as through
traffic from North to South was concerned, and that
thereafter the line between Forres and Keith would
become merely a feeder for the Inverness to Perth
line—as indeed it was already. They therefore fought
it strenuously and though unable to defeat it they did
get some safeguarding clauses put in the Act which
gave them the right to have a booking office at
Inverness, and which stated specifically that traffic
to and from the Great North should have rights,
powers and privileges equal in all respects to
those for Highland traffics, and that when called on
to do so by the Great North the Highland should
concur with them in fixing through rates. The High-

landers, however, were also safeguarded by the provision that they should get the same rate per mile for goods carried by Aberdeen and Keith as they did by their own line by Dunkeld.

Keith was to be the place where traffic between the two railways was to be exchanged, and that was to be the cause of much trouble in the future. The clauses of the 1856 Act by which the Railways were empowered to make working agreements which were repeated in the Act of 1860 were repealed at this time, so the separation of the two Companies was now complete.

While this battle was going on in the North another was being fought in the South. It will be remembered that the original plan of the Great North of Scotland Railway included a line down the Denburn valley from Kittybrewster to a junction with the then Aberdeen Railway at a point just South of where the Aberdeen Joint Station now stands. The construction of this line had been postponed on account of its cost, but the idea of a junction between the Great North and the line of the South had not been abandoned. When the Aberdeen Railway altered its approach from the South and the level of its station at Guild Street, arrangements were made to allow a junction still to be made, but there was a good deal of bickering about it at that time. In 1853 when the Great North line was being built, they made another effort to make the line but as they considered that the Aberdeen Railway would also benefit by the making of the junction they applied to them for assistance. Terms could not be arranged, so the matter dropped again and the Waterloo line was built, though it was only regarded as a temporary alternative. Another effort was made in 1857, but again the Great North failed to get what they considered was adequate assistance from the Southern Companies which they approached, so once again nothing was done. After that they seemed to have lost interest and were soon enlarging their terminal stations at Kittybrewster and Waterloo, which looked as if they meant to settle down in them for good and all.

This, however, was by no means to the liking of the Scottish North Eastern—as the old Aberdeen Railway had now become. They were at this time by no means pleased with their Northern neighbour for naturally they objected very strongly to its policy of sending all the traffic it could South by sea. Mutterings of the coming Highland storm had doubtless also reached their ears and, as the building of a Highland line would rob them of traffic as well as the Great North, by the early part of 1860 they were very anxious to get a junction made. They accordingly approached the Great North and several meetings were held and plans prepared, but there was a difference of opinion as to the probable cost, the Scottish North Eastern thinking that it could be done for a hundred thousand pounds, whereas the Great North considered that a new station would have to be made and that the cost of the whole business would be nearer double that figure, of which they would have to pay half. In the end the negotiations broke down because the Scottish North Eastern insisted that a Bill should be introduced in the Session of 1861, while the Great North declared that the final plans had been submitted

to them too late to allow proper consideration of them.
They promised to add clauses to a Bill they were themselves introducing in 1861 binding themselves to go
forward in the following year with a scheme which
was not to cost more than one hundred thousand
pounds, but the Scottish North Eastern mistrusted
them and decided to promote a scheme of their own.

This new proposal, which became known as the
Limpet Mill Scheme, was produced by a nominally independent Company called the Scottish Northern
Junction Railway (really controlled by the Scottish
North Eastern) who brought a Bill into Parliament for
the session of 1862 to empower them to construct a
railway, leaving the Scottish North Eastern's main line
at the Limpet Mill, about three miles north of Stonehaven, going up west of Aberdeen and joining the
Great North of Scotland at Kintore.   The total length
of the railway would have been twenty-two miles, and
its estimated cost about £150,000 (of which the Scottish North Eastern were to have provided £90,000).
The distance between Stonehaven and Kintore by this
line would have been four and a half miles shorter
than by way of Aberdeen.   There were to be two short
branches to form junctions with the Deeside railway
at Culter, so arranged that trains could run from the
Northern Junction to the Deeside Railway in a westerly direction and from the Deeside to the Northern
Junction in a northerly direction and, as has been seen
in the last Chapter, the Scottish North Eastern tried
unsuccessfully to get running powers over the Deeside between Aberdeen and Culter.

This proposed line was extremely unpopular in
Aberdeen, though Deeside and places to the North

welcomed prospects of a shorter route to the South.
The railway itself was not a particularly good one, as
it involved a good many steep gradients and sharp
curves.   The Great North naturally fought it tooth
and nail, but despite their opposition and that of the
Aberdeen Town Council, the Bill succeeded in passing.   However, on the Great North's offering to make
a junction at Aberdeen at their own expense if the
Bill were withdrawn, a clause was inserted suspended
its operation to January 1st, 1863, and for ever if they
succeeded in getting an Act for a line of their own
before September 1st of that year.

If the Limpet Mill scheme were not to proceed something had to be done quickly, and in the autumn of
1862 the Great North of Scotland produced their
scheme for a junction between the two railways. The
Denburn line, though offering the best route, was
likely to prove very expensive, so they produced an
alternative scheme which became known locally as the
"Circumbendibus" line.   This railway would have left
the Guild Street terminus of the Scottish North Eastern and followed that line for a very short distance
southwards before turning away to the southwest
where a steep climb of about a mile at 1 in 72 would
have commenced. Ati ts most westerly point this line
would have been about three-quarters of a mile from
the existing line at Union Bridge. Much of it at that
part would have been in a cutting deep enough to
allow it to pass under the various streets which had
to be passed at a depth of twenty feet, but even so it
was looked upon as a threat to the western end of the
city, though at that time much of the territory through
which it passed was not built over.   In addition to

this extensive cutting there would have been an embankment near Kittybrewster thirty-seven feet high and three furlongs in length. The total length of the railway would have been two miles seven furlongs and it was estimated to cost £125,000. It had obvious disadvantages and was even more unpopular than the Northern Junction line, its announcement being greeted by a positive howl of execration. Local opinion was indeed very strongly opposed to it, meetings of protest were held and ten thousand people signed a petition against it. The Great North was popularly supposed to have committed a fraud on the city as it was believed that the promised junction was to be a line down the Denburn valley which Aberdeen wanted. This, however, was hardly fair as the Great North had never specified any particular route which this line was to take.

Despite this opposition the Bill was duly deposited and came before Parliament in the Session of 1863. It was, however, clearly not such a good scheme as a railway through the Denburn Valley, and this fact was at once obvious to the House of Commons Committee which was considering the Bill. Moreover, the Committee realised that such a line could in fact be constructed without injustice to either of the Companies concerned. The northern Company were prepared to spend £125,000 on the Circumbendibus scheme. The southern Company had already undertaken to provide £90,000 towards the cost of the Limpet Mill scheme. Of this, about £10,000 had already been spent in the Parliamentary fight. It was therefore arranged that the Great North should put their £125,000 into the construction of a Denburn Valley

line, while the southern Company were to spend
£70,000 on the Junction and £10,000 on removing
from their existing station to a new one.   Thus the
best route could be got without any increased cost to
either Company.   Thanks to the efforts of the Chairman of the Committee, Mr. Michael Dobbyn Hassard,
M.P., this plan was agreed to, and for his efforts he
received a very warm letter of thanks from the Town
Council of Aberdeen.

Even now all the difficulties had not been overcome.
The Scottish North Eastern Company was to make
the line and it had the choice of five routes.   The one
it chose involved a tunnel which passed under the east
lodge of the Aberdeen Royal Infirmary.   To this the
Infirmary Court objected on the ground that the noise
of trains passing would disturb the patients and they
prepared to petition Parliament not to pass the Bill.
The Great North, to whom the railway and North end
of the new Joint Station were to belong, had never
wanted a tunnel and the Infirmary Court were
accused of allowing themselves to become that Company's tool.   In the end the Infirmary Court withdrew their opposition, but the course of the line was
diverted further east to meet their objection as far as
possible.

As soon as the Act was passed, work was started
and pressed on energetically.   The opening was de-
layed by the roof of the northern tunnel falling in after
it had been finished, but the line was finally opened
to traffic on November 4th, 1867.

This new approach down to Aberdeen from the
North was a steep one, being on a falling gradient of

WATERLOO GOODS STATION, ABERDEEN.

THE DENBURN LINE (UNDER CONSTRUCTION), ABERDEEN.

1 in 72 to within a quarter of a mile of the new station. It involved the making of two short tunnels, and the one at Hutcheon Street, though only 269 yards long, was the longest on the whole Great North system. It also involved the covering up of the Denburn, which was enclosed in a culvert on which the lines were laid. Most people must have forgotten the existence of the Burn until the culvert was opened in connection with the re-building of the joint station nearly fifty years later. The line, of course, was constructed as a double one.

The offices of the new station were contained in a granite block on the East side of the station and were probably fully adequate to the requirements of those days. Platform accommodation consisted of one long through platform and two bays at both North and South ends of the station, which led off the circulating area between the offices and the main platform. The circulating area and a short section of the platforms were covered by a large arched roof supported on the east by the station buildings and on the west by a heavy retaining wall. In addition to the lines serving the platforms there were two through running lines within the station proper and two outside on the west for goods traffic.

At the time of its construction the new station was a matter of great pride to its owners and was claimed to be one of the best stations in the country, a claim which those who only knew it at the end of its life might well have found hard to believe. It was, however, undoubtedly quite adequate for the traffic requirements of the day, though even then it must have suffered from the fact that its platforms were short, narrow and low.

Thus at the end of 1867 direct through communication between the South and the North of Aberdeen at last became possible and the old Waterloo Station and the line leading to it became relegated to goods traffic only.

As a counter-attack on the Scottish North Eastern for their Limpet Mill scheme the Great North had become interested in the Montrose and Bervie Railway, which had already been authorised but not constructed, and planned to extend it northwards to Stonehaven and southwards to Arbroath, where it would have connected with the Dundee and Arbroath Railway. They hoped to get running powers over the Scottish North Eastern between Stonehaven and Aberdeen, thus affording an alternative route from the South to Aberdeen. It was also hinted that a branch might be thrown out to the Deeside line, probably from Stonehaven to Banchory by the Slug Pass. This scheme was not taken very seriously in the North, where is earned the nickname of the "Kittywake Railway", and it was rejected by Parliament. The Montrose and Bervie section was, of course, ultimately constructed and became part of the North British Railway.

In 1866 a general consolidation of the railway system of the North East of Scotland was brought about by the amalgamation of all the small Companies with the Great North. Though powers to amalgamate them were obtained in that year the Banffshire was not

actually brought in till August 31st, 1867, and the
Morayshire remained independent till 1881, as they
considered that the Strathspey lines had not been
working long enough in 1866 to allow a fair estimate
to be made of the effect of their traffic on their (the
Morayshire's) receipts. As has been seen, the Deeside
Company was leased to the Great North at the time
that these amalgamations were made, so by the time
the through route to the South was working that Company had obtained undisputed possession of the North
Eastern Counties of Scotland.

A great change for the worse had, however, come
over their financial position. The prosperity which
had favoured their early years did not last long. The
opening of the direct route between Inverness and
the South had cost them the Mail contract and traffics
which together was estimated to have been the equiva-
lent of a five per cent. dividend. As the Highland
had joined the Clearing House they were forced to do
the same and lost a quarter of their receipts from
goods as a result. Some of the branches, too, were
proving a disappointment, particularly those North of
Keith. The Strathspey line in particular was very
unproductive.

Ninety-four thousand pounds had, moreover, been
spent on the branches without the sanction of Parliament and the traffics they had been expected to produce had been anticipated by the system of taking
credit for interest on advances to them whether it had
been earned or not. The bargain with the Deeside
was an expensive one and the money put into the ill-
starred "Kittywake" line looked like being lost. In the
early 'sixties dividends up to seven per cent. had been

paid on the original shares, but by 1865 when all
these chickens had come home to roost they vanished
altogether.

Foreseeing trouble, the Directors let it be known
that they would welcome an investigation by the
shareholders, and a Committee was accordingly appointed to enquire into the Company's affairs. This
report criticised a good many of the directors' actions
but not very severely and no immediate action was
taken except to get powers to abandon the Banffshire's proposed line from Portsoy to Port Gordon as
recommended by the Committee.

However, at the end of 1866, the Directors offered
to resign, and this offer was accepted, but as there was
a hope of an amalgamation with the Scottish North
Eastern Company they were asked to be retained in
office till that question should be settled. Nothing
came of it, so they resigned early in the following year.
Six of the old Directors were re-appointed, including
Mr. John Duncan, who then became Chairman. Six
new directors were elected, amongst whom was Mr.
William Ferguson, of Kinmundy, who later became
Chairman and who was so largely responsible for the
great improvements that took place in the railway
during the latter part of the nineteenth century.

CHAPTER FIVE.

PROGRESS.

THE new Board which had been elected in 1867 had to face the unpleasant task of putting the Company's finances in order. They were in a parlous state. By now £270,000 had been spent without the sanction of Parliament, £400,000 had been borrowed from the Banks on the security of shares in the Branches, and there was a floating debt of nearly £410,000 on which six per cent. had to be paid. To remedy this state of affairs they had to pursue a policy of strict economy as the House of Lords had refused to sanction their proposal to create pre-preference shares and so no further developments were possible for several years.

This need for economy probably accounted for the fact that the opening of the junction with the railways to the South did not result in any appreciable improvement in their train services. In the summer of 1868 the main line service still consisted of five trains each way a day to Keith, four of which went on to Elgin. The mail train in those days left at one o'clock in the afternoon and got to Keith at 3.25, and, for some reason, waited there till 4 o'clock before proceeding to Elgin, which was not reached till 5.40. The fastest train to Elgin was the 7 a.m. which got there at 11.45, with ten minutes at

Keith.   The time spent on the journey from Aberdeen
to Keith varied from 2 hours 25 minutes to 2 hours
50 minutes, and to Elgin from 4 hours 5 minutes to
4 hours 35 minutes.   Coming up, the mail left Elgin
at 7.20 in the morning and got to Aberdeen at 11.50,
leaving Keith at 9.10.   There were only three up trains
from Elgin, of which the mail was the fastest, the
slowest then taking 4¾ hours.   From Keith the fastest
train took two hours 38 minutes and the slowest
2 hours and 45 minutes.

The Highland Railway's services between Keith and
Inverness were no better.   They now regarded their
Keith to Forres line as a branch whose main purpose
was to feed their main line and its train services were
accordingly arranged to suit their main line trains
without consideration of the Aberdeen services.   The
through service provided by the two Companies was
as follows :—

DOWN.

			a.m	p.m.	p.m.
Aberdeen	depart	...	7.0	1.0	4.45
Keith	arrive	...	9.28	3.25	7.20
Keith	depart	...	9.40	4.10	7.30
Inverness	arrive	...	12.25	7.20	10.15

UP.

			a.m.	a.m.	p.m.	p.m.
Inverness	dep.	...	6.30	10.18	12.40	3.10
Keith	arr.	...	9.5	12.51	3.25	6.10
Keith	dep.	...	9.10	1.0	4.0	6.20
Aberdeen	arr.	...	11.50	3.45	6.38	9.0

The branches were no better off.   To Peterhead

the fastest train took 2 hours 35 minutes down and 2 hours 38 minutes up.   Alford could get nothing better than 1 hour and 55 minutes down and 2 hours 10 minutes up for the 30-mile journey, while Macduff (then still Gellymill) was $2\frac{1}{2}$ hours away and slightly longer coming back.   The Deeside line had to content itself with three through trains, of which the best took 2 hours 25 minutes to reach Ballater and the worst 3 hours 10 minutes.   The best up-train, however, managed to get through in 2 hours 10 minutes. There were two extra trains as far as Banchory, from which place the fastest then took 52 minutes.

During the early 'seventies the only addition to their system was the short section from Gellymill to Macduff—about three-quarters of a mile—which was opened July 1st, 1872.   This section included a station for Banff called Banff Bridge.   It was very small and this caused an outcry among the inhabitants which was so violent that a Board of Trade Inspector had to be sent down to pacify them!

Prudent management soon afterwards began to show results.   By 1875 the financial position had been restored.   The money spent without the sanction of Parliament had been repaid, the floating debt had been cleared off and the unpaid dividends on the 5% Preference Stock had been put to debentures.   Full dividends were now paid on the 5% Preference Stock and the $4\frac{1}{2}\%$ A Preference Stock, and 3% on the $4\frac{1}{2}\%$ B Preference Stock and on the original shares. When the branches had been amalgamated with the parent Company, the shares in them which it held were distributed among the original shareholders, who

received £143 worth of shares in addition to their
original £100, and by now the original £100 shares
stood at 208 in the market.

Main line traffic had increased and soon after
this the doubling of it was announced, and the work
was completed as far as Kintore in June 1880.

Mr. Duncan had resigned the Chairmanship of the
Company in 1872 though he remained a director till
his death three years later.   He was succeeded as
Chairman by Lord Provost Leslie, who held that position till he died in 1879.   His successor was Mr.
William Ferguson of Kinmundy, during whose term
of office the whole character of the Railway was radi-
cally changed.   In the following year Mr. Milne,
who had been General Manager since 1856, resigned
owing to failing health, but he lived for another
twelve years to enjoy his retirement.   In the same
year Mr. Ferguson, the Secretary, resigned and was
elected to the Board, as honour which he did not
enjoy long as he died in the following year.   The
offices of General Manager and Secretary were again
united in one man and to fill them came Mr. William
Moffatt from the North Eastern.   Later in the same
year Mr. A. G. Reid came from the same Company to
be the Great North's Superintendent of the Line, and
so by the end of 1880 the three people who played the
most important part in the transformation of the railway were at their posts.

The time was now fully ripe for a forward policy
and they were not long in starting it.   The first thing
to be done was to get the line in order.   The permanent way, stations, signals, and plant were all in a

bad state and in the next four years they spent nearly a quarter of a million in bringing their system up to date. Most of the permanent way at that time was laid with iron rails, much of it without fish plates. The re-laying of this was vigorously undertaken and in the next five years 142½ miles were relaid with steel rails. More crossing places were also put in and the doubling of the main lines was completed to Inveramsay.

Of course, not much could be done to improve the train services until these essential alterations had been carried out, though their improvement was badly needed. During the period of economy which was now ending, there had been little or no change, and the main line train services were still much as they had been at the beginning of it. The mail by this time managed to get to Keith in two and a quarter hours, but there was an even longer delay here than twelve years previously, so the arrival time in Elgin was not till 6.25. Elgin had one more up-train but, as one of these waited for an hour and forty minutes in Keith, it took a total time of 6¼ hours to get through to Aberdeen. Probably, however, there were good local reasons for this arrangement.

Nor had the Highland connections improved much. The connection with the mail from Aberdeen had been altered to leave Keith at 3.40 and reach Inverness at 6.25, thus giving a through service in 5 hours and 10 minutes as against 5 hours 25 minutes by the 7.10, which had been the best in 1868 and which remained unchanged in 1880. Other alterations made little difference in the service time except that the 6.30 a.m. from Inverness now left at 6.0 and so added 30

minutes to the journey. Travelling in the North East
of Scotland was still a grim business in 1880!

The service to Peterhead had, however, been considerably improved, all the down trains taking 2 hours
10 minutes and one up train doing it in the same time.
The other Northern branches showed no appreciable
change.

There was a slight beginning of a suburban service
in the shape of one down and two up-trains to Dyce
daily, taking twenty minutes on the journey. There
were then only three intermediate stations between
Aberdeen and Dyce—Kittybrewster, Woodside, and
Buxburn, as it was then called.

The Deeside line, however, came off best. Through
services had been increased to five trains each way to
Ballater, with one daily and two on Saturdays only
to Banchory. Though there had already been an
attempt at a quickened service, by running one train
each way non-stop between Aberdeen and Crathes,
it was in this year, 1880, that the first effort was made
to run a "Deeside Express." The speed was not very
heroic as it took $1\frac{1}{2}$ hours in each direction, with four
intermediate stops the down-train leaving at 4.30 in
the afternoon and the up-train at 8.8 in the morning.
The slow trains, too, were a good deal better than they
had been twelve years before, the down-trains varying from 1 hour 50 minutes to 2 hours 10 minutes, and
the up-trains from 1 hour 50 minutes to 3 hours and
20 minutes, the latter including a stop of 1 hour 12
minutes in Banchory.

In 1881 the Morayshire Railway was amalgamated
with the Great North which thus got a line entirely of

its own to Elgin. Under its old management the Great North had been content to hand over and receive traffic at Keith, but they now quite naturally decided to try and develop their own route and carry as much through traffic by it as they could. The Highland, however, equally naturally objected and insisted that Keith should be the only point of interchange. So the battle between the two Companies broke out again and was fought with extreme vigour for the next seventeen years.

At the same time it was decided to complete the railway system of their district. It will be remembered that the Banffshire had had a scheme to build a line from Portsoy to Port Gordon which for reasons which have already been explained was never built. But the populous coastal district of Banffshire could not for ever be left without railway communication, and in 1881 a Bill was introduced to make a line from Portsoy to Buckie. In the first of the many Parliamentary battles which were to be fought by the two Northern Railways during the next sixteen years it was strenuously opposed by the Highland, who were successful in getting it rejected.

Another Bill was introduced in the following session, this time to make a line along the whole of the coast to a junction with the Lossiemouth Branch just outside Elgin. This application was more successful and was duly approved by Parliament, the Highland in the same session getting powers to build a line from Keith to Portessie.

The line for which the Great North then obtained powers was always known as the Coast Line as it ran

close to the Moray Firth for practically the whole of
its length.   Where the line is actually in view of the
sea it is an extremely picturesque one; much of the
coast is rugged and fine distant views can be obtained
of the Sutherland and Caithness Hills on a clear day.
There were considerable engineering works involved,
particularly at Cullen where the railway was carried
over the old sea town by means of high embankments
and viaducts.   But its most important engineering
work was the crossing of the Spey.   The ground on
either side of the river near its mouth is very flat
and the bed of the river itself is constantly changing
over a pretty wide area.   It was consequently necessary to make a long bridge.   The bow spring girder
type was decided on, having a main span of 350 feet.
This was at the time of its construction and for many
years afterwards the longest span on any single line
bridge in the country.   The line has some sharp
curves and one or two short banks, some of which are
as steep as 1 in 80.

As the Highland would not meet them over the
question of transferring traffic at Elgin the Great
North began to consider the possibility of taking other
steps, and during the passage of the Bill through
Parliament they were given running powers over the
Highland line from Elgin to Forres despite the strenuous opposition of its owners.   The powers so given
were really useless because they were only to become
operative if and when the Highland made use of
similar running powers which they were given from
Elgin to Portsoy.   As the Highlanders did not want
these running powers and had no intention of using

them, the concession to the Great North was obviously worth nothing at all.

In the autumn of this year there occurred the worst disaster which ever took place on the Great North. In the evening of November 27th the Inverythan bridge carrying the Macduff line over the Aberdeen to Banff road near Auchterless collapsed while the 4 p.m. train from Macduff was crossing it. The train was a mixed one consisting of an engine, five or six goods trucks, a covered goods van, two third class coaches, a first class coach and a brake van, with the goods trucks in front as was the habit in those days. The engine and the first two or three trucks got safely across but the last wagons got derailed and one of them and the first third-class coach fell through the bridge to the road thirty feet below. These two vehicles were so badly smashed that they were indistinguishable from one another, and it was in this coach that all the casualties occurred. The second third-class coach also fell through but remained end up and its passengers were able to climb out. The first class coach remained suspended over the gap and the guard's van never left the rails. Altogether five people were killed and many were injured.

The Board of Trade Inspector who conducted the enquiry into this accident reported that it was due to an internal fault in the cast iron beam which broke. The beam had been in place ever since the bridge was erected in 1857 and the fault could not have been detected, so no blame attached to the Chief Engineer or any of his subordinates.

Relations with their Northern neighbours were now very strained and a new opportunity to renew the

attack soon presented itself. The Highland main line
in those days was still the original one opened in 1863
which reached Inverness from the South by a great
détour from Aviemore via Dava and Forres. It was
obvious that a shorter route could be obtained by
making a more direct line from Aviemore to Inverness. In the year 1883 a company called the Glasgow
and North Western backed by the North British proposed to make a line from Glasgow to Inverness up
the west coast and along the Caledonian Canal. The
Highland naturally fought this threat from the west
with all their might and the Bill was rejected. However, during the fight in Committee the Highland
Chairman had undertaken to make the direct line
from Aviemore to Inverness and in the autumn of
1883 plans were prepared and their intention to seek
powers to build the line was announced.

The Great North's Chairman had also had his eye
on this bit of country—a fact probably not unknown
in Inverness—and as soon as this announcement was
made the Great North suggested that it should be a
joint line between the two enterprises. This proposal
was immediately rejected, so the Great North produced a scheme for a line of their own. This would
have left their Strathspey line immediately after it
crossed the Spey and just before its junction with the
Highland line.   It was proposed to put in another
junction with that line where the proposed new line
crossed it.   From there it would have gone north and
after crossing the Dulnan River turned West by Duthil
to Carr Bridge. After that it would have followed more
or less the same line as that proposed by the Highland, the most important difference being the ap-

100 Years Ago This Engine Was Built

The Glengrant finished its days on the Oldmeldrum line.

NE hundred years ago last week Mrs Grant, wife of ...es Grant, an Elgin banker joint proprietor of the ...nlivet Distillery, Rothes, ...the first sod for the laying ...railway between Elgin and ...siemouth.

...e line was planned by an ...neer named Samuel, who at ...time was constructing the ...from the south to Aberdeen.

...e first train ran over the ...n-Lossiemouth line on Aug. ...852, two months before the ...tish North-eastern Railway ...pany had trains running in ...out of Aberdeen.

...muel also designed two ...nes and named one Glen-...t and the other Lesmurdie.

...engines, carriages and goods ...ons arrived at Lossiemouth ...oat.

...mes Ross, a Ross-shire man,

and William Walker, an Elgin labourer, who were driving horses and carts on the track, were asked to try their hands at driving the engines. They were proud of their jobs and received £1 a week for a sixteen-hour working day.

The Elgin-Lossiemouth Railway remained a popular and paying one until the arrival of motor buses in 1919. Since then it has been a struggle to maintain passenger traffic, and many think the railway will not celebrate its hundredth birthday next August.

The Glengrant engine finished its days on the Inverurie to Oldmeldrum branch line.

A crash at Porston, when a traction engine dropped on to the line through a wooden bridge nearly half a century ago, was the finish of the Glengrant.

ome so dear in the U.S. that looking elsewhere for sup- kesmen in Chicago.

Mr F. Houser, vice-president of Sears Roebuck, world's biggest mail-order house, who is just back from a five-week trip to Britain, announced that his company would immediately set up buying offices in France and Germany.

"British textiles are too high for our wants."

Mr Joel Goldblatt, president of Goldblatt Department Stores, operating a chain of fifteen stores in Chicago and the Middle West, complained:—"British goods are over-priced."

He was sending his chief buyer to Tokio in the spring with samples "from bicycles to gloves to see what Japanese manufacturers can do."

Britain Replies

Mr David Mayer, president of Maurice Rothschild and Co., a leading high-quality store in the Middle West, said:—"Our stores are anxious to promote British goods, but the prices are making it difficult to sell the merchandise. We did very well with British tweed suits at about £28, but now we would have to sell the same suits at about £3/10/- more.

"Customers are resisting these prices, and I cannot take a chance on stocking suits at these prices."

A Board of Trade spokesman said last night: "We believe British exporters are fully conscious of the importance of keeping their prices in the American market as competitive as they can. Signs of marked sales resistance among the American public to British goods have not been apparent so far."

---

gave evidence against the nu

Infuriated Crow

One of the witness's testir was lost in shouts from crowd. And so it went on. accusation increased the fu the crowd. Finally the judge called for order and that the verdict was up to people.

Spectators then told the what they thought should done with the accused. Afte hour of suggestions and flammatory speeches, the furiated crowd almost got o hand.

"No, don't beat them yet," judge was heard to cry as sentences were announced.

A commentator broke in a point to describe how each walked round the circular bowing and apologising fo "crimes." The crowd roare

And there was still no from the nuns. If anybody fended them, his voice was heard. If they were giver opportunity to defend themse they were not heard.

After 42 Year

The nuns were arrested in March this year. While were held incommunicad propaganda campaign ag them in China increased.

With the arrest of the nuns, seven remaining Cana nuns applied for exit visa Hong-Kong, and thus end period of forty-two years' se by their order in Canton.

John Norga to Be Free

JOHN ROBERT NORGAN w released from Bruges Pri the end of this month, his co Maitre Van Parijs, said yest cables Gavin Gordon from Br

"It is all fixed," he added will be a conditional releas condition being that he leave gium straight away."

Norgan's sentence, origina life, was red

proach to Inverness, the Great North's coming down much more steeply than that proposed by the Highland.

As a through route from Aberdeen to Inverness this line would have suffered from the double disadvantage of being longer than the Highland's existing one— 130 miles as compared with 108—and also being a much more difficult one to work as it passed through a mountainous instead of a comparatively flat country. The existing Strathspey line, too, was not well suited to form part of a through line as it had many sharp curves and steep gradients. As part of a through route from Inverness to the south it also suffered from the grave objection that it would have brought two companies into the working of a line which obviously ought to belong to one.

The Great North's proposal was not really a very good one and they can hardly have seriously expected Parliament to prefer it to that of their rivals. The Highland roundly accused them of bringing it forward as a piece of blackmail to get other terms out of them, to which they replied that the Highland had only brought forward this scheme to keep them out and that if they did get powers they would be in no hurry to use them—a prophecy which proved very accurate.

Both Bills came before the same Committee of the House of Commons in the following year, but not unnaturally the Committee preferred the Highland scheme, which was passed and that of the Great North rejected. The latter Company did, however, succeed in convincing Parliament that the Highland's treat-

ment of their traffic was not all that it should
be and certain Conciliation Clauses were inserted
in the Highland's Act which stated that both Companies should provide proper facilities for the
exchange of traffic at any junctions on their systems,
such facilities to include "through bookings by
tickets and invoices and so far as may be reasonably required through carriages, wagons and trucks
and conveniently timed and arranged trains, whether
ordinary or special, as the case may require by any
junction". It was also provided that "each Company
shall from time to time duly receive and transmit on
or over their railways and deliver all such traffic passing or intended or directed to pass to the railway of
the other of them effectively, regularly and expedi-
tiously and in all respects on an equality with their
own proper traffic or as if it were traffic which they
were desirous of cultivating to the utmost." These
clauses and particularly the reference to "any junction" seemed adequate and with them for the time
being the Great Northern had to be content.

By the same Act powers were conferred on the
Great North to build a railway from Fraserburgh to
Roseharty but they were never used.

In this same year 1884 a very ambitious project
was brought forward by some Deeside and Donside
landowners under the leadership of the late Marquis
of Huntly. This was for a line to connect Speyside
with Deeside and was known as the Strathspey,
Strathdon and Deeside Junction Railway. Starting
from a Junction with the Great North's Speyside line
just east of Nethybridge Station it would have turned

south and, using the valleys of the Dorbach, Brown
and Alnack burns, reached the Avon well above Tomintoul. From the Avon Valley the head waters of the
Don were to be reached by a tunnel 3,190 yards long.
On its course down the Don valley it would have
crossed that river three times and passed through
two tunnels before turning up the Deskrie Burn to
reach Deeside. The pass between the Don and the
Dee at this point is a high one and to get down to the
Deeside railway the proposed line would have had to
make a great loop following the hill sides. The junction with the Deeside line would have been about half
a mile east of Cambus o'May station. The total
length of this proposed Railway would have been 42
miles. It would have included four tunnels of a total
length of 5,150 yards, its summit level would have been
1,500 feet above the sea—and so the highest of any
British railway—and it would have contained many
very steep gradients of which the worst was a four
mile bank at 1 in 56 immediately after leaving the
Speyside line. The estimated cost was £600,000.

The Great North of Scotland informed its promoters that they would not be prepared to subscribe anything to its construction though it appears that they
had subscribed a small amount towards the initial
costs and would have been prepared to work it once
it was constructed. Parliament, however, decreed
otherwise and no more was heard of it.

From a scenic point of view this would have been a
magnificent line. But where its traffic was to come
from is not so obvious. The district through which
it would have passed was very sparsely populated so

there was no hope of local traffic, though its promoters attached considerable importance to the granite of Culblean and a deposit of iron ore in the Upper Strathdon. Except as a tourist route in summer it had few possibilities.

It is not easy after a lapse of fifty years to understand why the Highlands of Scotland held out such attractions to would-be railway builders towards the end of last century, yet not only private individuals but the Scottish Railways fell victims to this allurement. The Highland which was there knew all about its limitations, but the Great North of Scotland on the one side and the North British on the other seemed to have altogether exaggerated ideas of the value of Highland traffic. It is true that there was a very rich tourist traffic for some three months in the year, but beyond that there was little but sheep and fish—hardly enough, one would think, to make fat dividends. However, in the 'eighties and 'nineties of last century these two railways evidently thought the game was worth playing and played it vigorously.

The Highland having got powers to build their short line were in no hurry to make use of them, nor were they, in the Great North's view, any more anxious to give effect to the Conciliation Clauses inserted in their Act. A violent quarrel over the timing of a train—in which the Highlands' action was, to say the least, vexatious—led to an application in 1885 by the Great North to the Board of Trade to compel the Highland to run two trains a day from Inverness to Elgin to connect with their trains there. The Commissioners' finding was not at all satisfactory to the

Great North as though it made orders on both Companies to run trains it fixed Keith as the point of exchange. They accordingly applied for a re-hearing, which was granted though not on the question of the point of the exchange of traffic. It was, however, never held as the two Managers decided to try and come to an arrangement between themselves, and in 1886 an agreement covering the points at issue was reached which was to last for seven years. Under it all matters in dispute were to be referred to an arbiter who was at first Mr. Grierson of the Great Western and later Mr. Tennant of the North Eastern. So for a short time there was comparative peace.

The Great North in the meantime had made steady progress on their own system. Relaying the line was progressing rapidly as the directors very properly attached great importance to this. New sidings at Kittybrewster had been completed in 1883 and they proved an immense help in dealing with the growing traffic. Double line had reached Inveramsay in 1882 and Cults on the Deeside line in 1884.

In 1884 the third class fares were reduced to a penny a mile. Apparently the Company was encouraged to do this by the fact that passenger duty on penny-a-mile fares was withdrawn at about this time. The third class carriages were also being improved— the old ones were partitioned and the seats upholstered while new and improved ones were introduced. As a result of all this third class travellers increased in numbers considerably, and already there were complaints at the half-yearly meeting of a falling off in "Firsts".

Train services were also improved and July 1885 saw the introduction of the first express from Aberdeen to Elgin. It seems to have been put on as an action in the above-mentioned quarrel with the Highland, but in July 1885 the East and West Coast Companies started running trains from London at 8 p.m. which reached Aberdeen at 9.55 a.m. which probably also accounted for it. It left Aberdeen at 10.10 a.m. and reached Keith at 11.50 and Elgin at 1.0 p.m. There was no corresponding up-train till the next year. It was originally meant to connect at Elgin with the Highland train put on that summer from Keith at 12.25, but as soon as it appeared the Highlanders altered their train to run twenty minutes earlier to ensure a connection at Keith only! The arrival time at Inverness, needless to say, remained the same—2.45!

In August the Great North accelerated this train by four minutes to Keith and ten minutes to Elgin and in September the Highland put on a fast connection from Keith which left at 11.50 and reached Inverness at 1.30 calling only at Fochabers (now Orbliston Junc.), Elgin, Alves, Forres and Nairn. This was the only down express ever run between Aberdeen and Inverness by the two companies via Mulben and was also the fastest down train ever provided by them between those places.

Improved services had also by now been given to the Branches—chiefly on the smaller ones—by the separation of passenger and goods trains. Thus Alford could be reached in one hour and twenty minutes, Macduff in two hours five minutes, and

Peterhead in two hours. The Deeside trains had also
been improved and the expresses on that section now
took an hour and a quarter down and seventy-two
minutes up.

The first section of the coast line had been opened
as far as Tochieneal on the 1st April, 1884, and a section at the other end from Garmouth to Elgin on the
12th August of the same year. The intervening
stretch which contained all the really heavy engineering works was not, however, opened until 3rd May,
1886. At this same time there was opened a new loop
line at Grange to enable trains from the south to proceed directly to the coast. Previously they had to go
into Grange Station and reverse there. The opening
of the through route also involved another alteration
in working. Banff had up till then been the terminus
of the main line and the section from Tillynaught to
Portsoy had been worked as a Branch. This arrange-
men now had to be reversed—the Tillynaught-Banff
section becoming the branch and the Portsoy section
the main line.

Just a year after the new line was opened there was
a serious accident, luckily unaccompanied by loss of
life. It will be remembered that at Cullen the line is
carried over the Sea Town by a series of viaducts and
embankments. One of the latter slipped and so
caused a collapse of two arches of a viaduct. As a
result the line was closed altogether for fifteen days.
In the end the two collapsed arches were replaced by
an embankment and the third arch of the viaduct was
filled in with concrete, and no further trouble was
experienced.

With the opening of the Coast line an express connection was given off the 10.10 a.m. from Aberdeen
reaching Elgin at 12.55. An up express had started
to run on January 1st, 1886, leaving Elgin at 1.40 p.m.
and reaching Aberdeen at 4.20 p.m. To this train a
connection by the Coast was also given leaving Elgin
at 1.35 p.m. At Aberdeen a connection was made with
the English mail which left at 4.40 p.m. Altogether
there were five trains each way between Aberdeen and
Elgin by the new route while there were six down and
seven up trains between Aberdeen and Keith. In July
of this year the Highland's fast 11.50 a.m. from Keith
was withdrawn and a train was run from Elgin in
connection there with the 10.10 from Aberdeen which
reached Inverness at 2.15, so the fast down service was
short lived. An up train now left Inverness at 12
noon to connect with the afternoon express to Aberdeen at Elgin—these Elgin connections probably being the result of the Agreement come to between the
Companies earlier in the year.

The full through service between Aberdeen and
Inverness was now as follows :—

	a.m.	a.m.	a.m.	p.m.	p.m.
Aberdeen dep. ...	3.35	7.0	10.10	1.15	4.55
Inverness arr. ...	8.5	11.50	2.15	6.5	10.5

	a.m.	noon	p m.	p.m.
Inverness dep. ...	6.0	12.0	3.0	4.0
Aberdeen arr. ...	11.35	4.20	7.0	9.30

A fast train was also now run on the Buchan line
leaving Aberdeen at 10.15 and reaching Peterhead at
11.55 and Fraserburgh at 12 noon. The return train
left Peterhead at 2.45 (Fraserburgh 2.40) and reached

Aberdeen at 4.25. There were altogether five trains each way on this section, the slow ones taking from 2 hours 5 minutes to 2 hours 15 minutes.

In the following year Aberdeen got its first suburban services. There was an increasing industrial population up the valley of the Don between Aberdeen and Dyce which might provide a useful source of income if given a good service. Accordingly in July 1887 a start was made to develop this traffic. New stations were opened at Bankhead and Stoneywood and a service of eight local daily trains were provided. The time taken was twenty minutes. During the next six months other stations were opened at Don Street and Hutcheon Street. By the beginning of 1888 the service had been increased to 12 each way. The time allowed remained 20 minutes despite the extra stops, and it was never subsequently changed though two more stations were added later—Persley between Woodside and Buxburn and Schoolhill, which was barely a quarter of a mile from the north end of the Aberdeen Joint station. For many years this was a very popular service, but later it suffered from the competition of trams and it was finally killed in 1937 by motor buses after a life of nearly fifty years.

In 1888 another express in each direction was added between Aberdeen and Elgin taking 2 hours and 40 minutes on the journey. The up train ran non-stop from Huntly to Aberdeen, 40¾ miles in 68 minutes, which was then and for many years after the longest non-stop run on the system. In this year also the up 5 p.m. train from Keith was accelerated to reach Aberdeen at 6.50 and thus for the first time the journey from Inverness to Aberdeen could be made in less than four hours.

The main line had been doubled as far as Insch by the autumn of 1888, but this still left two-thirds of the Coast line to Elgin and practically all the rest of the system single.   One of the most serious disadvantages of single line working for express trains was the fact that they had to slow up at each crossing place to exchange the tablet or staff.   Moreover, the exchanging of tablets by hand also frequently resulted in injuries to the staff.   Most of the Great North system was then still worked on the old system of telegraphic passing orders, but the Coast Line had been equipped with the tablet system.   To overcome the disadvantage of fast trains having to slow up at each crossing place, and more particularly to avoid injuries to the staff, Mr. Manson, who was then the locomotive superintendent, decided to try and find a mechanical means of exchange.

The first apparatus tried was similar to that already in use for the exchange of mail bags.   This however did not prove satisfactory so another method was sought.   There was at that time at Kittybrewster a blacksmith, Mr. John Duncan, and Mr. Manson consulted him.   He had previously been employed at Broadford Works where he had seen an apparatus which transferred cotton from one machine to another. This operation was patented, but he got permission to examine it and proceeded to experiment on similar lines.   From this came the finally successful tablet exchange apparatus.

It consisted of two parts—one on the ground and

the other on the engine. The one on the ground consisted of a metal post fitted with a moveable arm which could be pushed forward or drawn back by a hand lever. On this arm are fixed two forks, one facing the direction in which the train is coming and the other that in which it is going. The other part of the machine is on the engine and consists of an arm with two similar forks set at such a height that they will just pass over the ones on the ground machine. The tablets are enclosed in a strong flat leather pouch. The one to be picked up by the train is inserted in the forward fork of the machine on the ground and held in place by strong springs. As the train approaches the signalman who is in charge of this machine having inserted the tablet in the appropriate fork moves the forks forward by means of the lever and they are now in a position which brings them immediately under those on the engine. The tablet to be dropped is inserted in the rear fork of the engine's machine, the forward fork of which picks up the tablet from the ground machine whose backward fork simultaneously catches the tablet suspended from the corresponding fork on the engine. The engine's machine when not in use is kept conveniently inside the cab. To avoid inaccurate setting the turntable at Kittybrewster is fitted with a gauge by which any machine can readily be tested.

This ingenious machine was first used in public in May 1889. At first the men were naturally cautious and tablets were only exchanged at quite low speeds—15 miles an hour or so—but with greater experience the men gained confidence in the new machine and before very long they were using it at full speed. It

was subsequently erected at all crossing places on the
Great North Railway all of whose engines were fitted
with their portion of it.   It was also adopted by the
Highland Railway and has been in use on those two
systems ever since. To his eternal honour Mr. Manson
refused to patent it because he did not want to put any
possible hindrance in the way of the adoption of any
machine the use of which would increase the safety of
the men.

CHAPTER SIX.

OPTIMISM.

T HE "Naughty Nineties" as they are sometimes called were to prove the period of the Great North's most rapid and vigorous development, but they began with a set back.

The agreement come to with the Highland Railway in 1886 was not working well and there was constant friction between the two Companies. The Great North accordingly decided to make a fresh effort to get to Inverness. This time they planned a simultaneous frontal and flanking attack on the enemy's capital. In the session of 1890 they applied to Parliament for powers to construct a line of their own from Elgin to Inverness and also one through the Black Isle from Fortrose by Munlochy to a junction with the Highland's Northern main line at Muir of Ord. The Black Isle line was to be connected with the Elgin to Inverness line by a ferry service across the Moray Firth. They also sought powers to build a line from Elgin to Burghead by Hopeman.

The new line to Inverness was to cross the existing Highland line by a bridge almost in Elgin Station and then to proceed in a south-westerly direction following the valley of the Black Burn south of Eildon Hill, and thence to Forres by way of Rafford. It was to keep to the South of the Highland line till Nairn where it crossed it again to reach the coast just south of Campbeltown. At this point there was to be the southern ferry pier, the northern one being at the west end of Fortrose. From Campbeltown the new line was to keep between its rival and the sea to Inverness.

This scheme was, of course, opposed by the Highland, who were again successful in warding off the attack. Their defence was that the existence of the agreement of 1886 made such a measure unnecessary. The Committee of the House of Commons agreed with them and found that the preamble of that part of the bill which proposed to make the new line from Elgin to Inverness not proved, whereupon the Great North withdrew the whole Bill.

The attack, however, was not entirely without result. The Highland could hardly face such a Parliamentary contest and declare that no further facilities for the Inverness traffic were required when they had done nothing to make use of the powers they possessed to make their new cut off from Aviemore, so in December 1889 they called for tenders for its construction, which was commenced in the following year.

The year 1890 was notable in British Railway history for a much more important event than the Great North's defeat in their effort to get to Inverness. The Forth Bridge was opened in that year and at once the whole Scottish Railway situation was changed. The East Coast partners now had their own route to Perth and Aberdeen which was shorter by many miles than their old one, and which now became the shortest from London to all the North of Scotland.

The Great North had some hopes that this would work out to their advantage. Speaking at the half-yearly meeting in September, 1889, their Chairman said : "The East Coast might easily bring in a train leaving London at 7.45 or 8 p.m. to Aberdeen at 7.30 a.m., the hour at which the Highland leaves Perth. We here are only 124 miles from Inverness over a good road, a large portion of which is double line, while Perth is 144 miles of mountainous and single line. There would be no difficulty then in allowing ample time for breakfast in Aberdeen and still landing passengers at Inverness sooner than they can go there by the West Coast and Highland mail as at present run. But these are speculations. They will, however, soon now be tested by actual experience."

This was not the first time that they had put forward the idea that they might form the northern end of the East Coast Route to Inverness as they had also suggested it when they were trying to get their Carr Bridge line five years earlier. Their hope of achieving this may have been another reason for their renewed effort to get a line of their own to the Highland Capital. It was a vain hope. An East Coast and Great North route to Inverness would have been fully fifty-five miles longer than that of the West Coast and Highland combination, and it was altogether too optimistic to hope that the North British would not want to make the utmost use of their new Glenfarg line to Perth or that the West Coast partners would be content to allow their rivals to get all the Aberdeen traffic by such much faster trains.

I

What actually happened was that in the summer of 1890 the East Coast got their 8 p.m. train from London to Aberdeen at 8.0 the next morning and the West Coast got theirs at 9.0 This allowed the Great North to start their train to the North earlier and it was accordingly altered to leave at 9.30, but the running was actually slightly slower than before as it reached Elgin at 12.12 via the Coast line and 12.13 via Craigellachie. Inverness was not reached till 1.35, the connection being made by Mulben.

By the following year the Highland were getting their London passengers by both routes to Inverness by 11.5 a.m., and away to the North at 11.25—long before this 1.35 arrival by Aberdeen—a sad disappointment to the Great North's hopes of the Forth Bridge!

The Caledonian now ran a train from Aberdeen to Glasgow and London at 5.40 p.m. and the up afternoon express from Elgin was altered to leave at 2.25 by both routes and reach Aberdeen at 5.15 which was again a slowing.   On the other hand the up morning express had five minutes taken off its time and the up evening fast from Keith was accelerated by the same amount of time to reach Aberdeen at 6.45, in time—but only just in time—to connect with North British and Caledonian trains to the South, which now left at 6.50 and 7 p.m. respectively.

Corresponding alterations were also made in the fast Buchan trains, the down train being now due to leave Aberdeen at 9.25 a.m. and arrive at Peterhead at 11.5 a.m. and Fraserburgh at 11.10 a.m., the up train leaving Fraserburgh at 3.35 and Peterhead at

3.40, reaching Aberdeen at 5.20 p.m.. which latter times remained unchanged till the Great War.

In 1891 the Great North started into a new line of business by taking over the Palace Hotel in Aberdeen. It had been built in 1874 by Messrs. Pratt & Keith, who occupied the shops on the ground floor, but at the time the railway took it over the hotel part was in the hands of a private concern. The newcomers promptly set about modernising it and putting in electric light —a very modern idea for 1891—and reopened it in August of that year. A covered way was provided from the station, a roof being put on the main North platform for its whole length, access from there to the various parts of the hotel being given by a covered bridge over the lines and two hydraulic lifts in the building.

From the start it was a financial success and this may have encouraged the Great North in its next venture in hotel keeping. In 1893 powers were obtained to build an hotel and make a golf course at Cruden Bay on the Aberdeenshire Coast about twenty miles North of Aberdeen. The site was ideal —a fine bay with a magnificent sandy beach—a perfect place in which to make a golf course but there was no railway nearer than Ellon, a full ten miles away over a comparatively poor piece of country. So the plan included the making of the necessary line which was also continued on beyond Cruden Bay for about five miles to the small fishing town of Boddam. It was a disastrous undertaking. The Hotel was very comfortable and the golf course soon got the reputation of being one of the best in

Scotland, but the season was too short to make them profitable and the railway never paid—indeed, it was always run at a loss and the time was to come when all concerned wished it had never been made.

Everything in the Great North's garden in the early 'nineties must have looked particularly rosy for this was not the only over-ambitious scheme which was launched at that time.   The locomotive works which were then at Kittybrewster were very cramped and far too small—indeed, much of the work had to be done in the open.   How Mr. Manson managed to build two engines there—which he did in 1887—is a marvel.   To provide better accommodation it was decided to move the whole works lock, stock and barrel to Inverurie, fifteen miles away on the main line. Here again the directors may have been influenced by success for they estimated that they had saved about £300 to £400 on the two engines built at Kittybrewster, and they may have been encouraged by the thought of similar savings on all their engines if they could build them in works of their own.   Perhaps had they realised that it would be nearly 20 years before any engine was built there they might have thought differently.   Be that as it may, they decided on the change and got powers to take the necessary land.

One very valuable move, however, was made at this time.   The offices of the Company were then where they had always been, at the old Waterloo Station. This must have been very inconvenient for not only were they badly situated there but they were very cramped and inadequate in themselves.   A new site was therefore procured in Guild Street, from which a

Up Train at Cruden Bay Station.

side entrance could be provided straight into the North end of the Joint Station and here a new and handsome block of offices was erected. It was opened in 1894 and was in every way worthy of a much larger and more opulent Company than the Great North. The wisdom of this move has never been questioned for its advantages were too obvious.

In other directions sound progress was being made. Main line services were developed and in 1892 under a ruling by the arbiter appointed by the agreement of 1886 a fast service was given between Aberdeen and Inverness daily in each direction by Elgin. The up train left Inverness at 9.0 a.m., Nairn at 9.25, and Forres at 9.45, and reached Elgin at 10.10. The Great North train was put back to leave at 10.20, but the arrival time at Aberdeen remained 12.55. The return service was in the evening, the down express from Aberdeen being altered to leave at 6.40 p.m. instead of 7.0 and to reach Elgin at 9.20 p.m. The Highland connection left Elgin at 9.30, reaching Forres at 9.55, Nairn at 10.15 and Inverness at 10.40. This service was short lived for when the agreement was ended in the following year the Highland withdrew their trains because they said they did not pay. The Great North train then had several more stops added and its arrival at Elgin put back to 9.35 p.m.

In 1894 there was further improvement. A new fast morning train was put on from Keith to Aberdeen, but it was timed to start at exactly the same time as the Highland train from Inverness was due to arrive—doubtless a case of the Great North getting some of their own back, but it must have been mad-

dening for the passengers who had to continue their
journey by the old slow 8.35, which did not get to
Aberdeen till 11.0, whereas the new express arrived
at 9.55.   The down afternoon train which had been
badly slowed some years before was also quickened
again and got through to Keith as a semi-fast in an
hour and fifty-five minutes.   By an interesting alteration in its running times the up morning express was
now timed to reach Aberdeen in sixty-three minutes
from Huntly, including a conditional stop at Dyce and
a ticket stop at the new Schoolhill Station, which had
been opened at the end of the previous year.   The
allowance of forty-eight minutes from Huntly to the
Dyce conditional stop involving an average speed of
43.1 miles per hour was distinctly good, particularly
when it is remembered that at that time double line
only extended to Insch.

The through service between Aberdeen and Inverness in the summer of 1894 was as follows :—

		a.m.	a.m.	a.m.	p.m.	p.m.	p.m.
Aberdeen	dep.	3.30	6.50	9.30	1.15	5.30	
Keith	arr.	5.15	9.0	11.10	3.30	7.50	
	dep.	5.25	9.7	11.20	3.35	8.0	
Inverness	arr.	8.10	11.5	1.35	6.5	10.5	
Inverness	dep.	6.0	8.45	10.10	12.40	3.0	3.45
Keith	arr.	8.25	11.10	12.15	3.20	4.50	6.20
	dep.	8.35	11.20	12.55	3.30	5.0	7.30
Aberdeen	arr.	11.0	12.55	3.15	5.15	6.45	9.30

Of these only one down train, the 9.30, gave a connection at Elgin but four up trains did so—the 8.45
and 10.10 a.m., 12.40 and 3.45 p.m.   Through carriages, however, were all sent by Keith, though the
8.45 a.m. up train also had one via the Coast.

Important developments had also been taking place on the Deeside line. Soon after suburban services had been started between Aberdeen and Dyce there was a demand for such a service on Deeside. The railway, however, did not at that time feel that they could give this as they wanted some experience of the working of the new service first. Moreover, the Deeside line was at that time only double as far as Cults and a suburban service could not be worked over a single line, and even then there were doubts as to whether such extra trains could be accommodated in the Aberdeen Joint station. The circumstances, too, were different for whereas in the Don Valley there was an established and rapidly growing manufacturing and commercial population, that on Deeside was purely residential.

Such a service, however, had great possibilities. The Dee Valley near its mouth is an ideal place for the residential suburbs of a great city. On the North side the hills rise steeply enough to afford good protection and yet gently enough to make building on them possible. The valley is wide and the views to the South are, therefore, expansive and beautiful. Everything pointed to continued development. By the end of 1892 the line had been doubled to Culter and in 1894 a suburban service was started to that place—two new stations, Holburn Street and Pitfodels being opened at the same time. The service consisted of 10 down trains and nine up, taking 21 minutes down and 22 up, a standard time which was never changed throughout the whole life of this service. The down trains to Ballater were then relieved of their suburban stops, reaching Culter in 14 minutes non stop. The

up trains, however, continued to call at several suburban stations and this arrangement was continued
with one exception till the War.

By now the Culter viaduct—over which there had
been a restriction to 15-20 m.p.h.—had been strength-
ened and at the other end of the line the prohibition
on all except the lightest locomotives from working
between Aboyne and Ballater which had been in force
for some years had also been removed.

Most important of all the developments of these
years, however, was the introduction of the Block system over the whole railway in January 1893. After
this the tablet exchange apparatus spread from the
coast to other sections so the Great North was well
equipped for the faster train services which were
gradually being instituted.

While these domestic developments were taking
place the battle with the Highland was not allowed
to flag and during the early 'nineties they made
two indirect attempts to get to Inverness. Away in
Wester Ross is the town of Ullapool on Loch Broom
which hoped that given better communication with the
rest of the world its fishing industry might revive. In
1890 a concern known as the Garve and Ullapool Railway got powers to construct a railway between those
two places. Garve is on the Highland Railway's
Dingwall and Skye Branch, and the new line was to
have been worked by them. The Company, however,
could not raise the necessary money or come to an
agreement with the Highland for its construction with
the help of a Government subsidy. Accordingly in
1892 with the Great North's consent they brought for-

ward a Bill to transfer their powers to that Company, who were to get running powers over the Highland line from Elgin to Garve. Negotiations were opened with the Treasury, but they came to nothing and the Bill was dropped. An Act authorising the abandonment of the railway was obtained in 1893.

In that year another company with the backing of the Great North sought powers to make a railway from Achnasheen, also on the Skye line, along Loch Maree and by way of Gareloch and Pool Ewe to Aultbea on the north side of Loch Ewe. Needless to say, the Great North again sought running powers over the Highland to give them access to their far off protégé. But once again they failed, for the Bill did not pass. Though doubtless both these railways would have been of great advantage to the districts they proposed to serve, the chances of their bringing an adequate return to their promoters were very remote. To the Great North, however, their value was that through them they could get running powers over the Highland and so reach Inverness.

The agreement between the Great North and Highland railways was terminable in the summer of 1893 and early in that year the Highland gave notice that they proposed so to terminate it. The reason they gave for so doing was that under it receipts for all traffic between Grange and Elgin for traffic to and from places south of Grange and west of Elgin were to be pooled, each company getting half of such receipts. The Great North thereupon handed over all such traffic at Keith and so got their share of the profits without having done anything to earn them! Why the Highland should not have retaliated by handing over traffic in the other direction at Elgin and so getting the same advantage does not appear. The truth was that the agreement had worked badly. During the period in which it had been in operation one hundred and eight cases had been brought before the arbiters by the Great North and ninety-one by the Highland. Though most of the points at issue had been cleared up there were still some outstanding at the end of the period. The Great North still had to fight to get any concessions and with the termination of the agreement, things from their point of view went from bad to worse.

In all spheres of human activity personality plays an important part and it seems to have done so in this case. Mr. Dougall, the General Manager of the Highland Railway, had held that office in the old Aberdeen and Inverness Junction Company, and he seems never to have got over a dislike of the Great North formed in those early days; and to judge by some of his letters to that Company he was hardly of a conciliatory nature. On the other hand, Mr. Moffatt of the Great North was certainly no man of peace—at any rate where Highlanders were concerned—and as long as those two were in control of their respective companies relationships were bound to be difficult.

At this time the Highland were at last getting on with their new short line from Aviemore and there were rumours of a new line from Fort William up the Caledonian Canal to Inverness as well. The combined effect of all this was that the Great North prepared a Bill for the session of 1894 by which they sought to get running powers between Elgin and Inverness. But the Highland made some steps to meet them and the Fort Augustus line disappeared, so the Bill was dropped. However, the Highland's steps were not very long ones and the Fort William line again appeared, so the Great North revived their Bill for the session of 1895.

In this venture they had the backing of several important independent bodies. The Town Council of Aberdeen were not unnaturally unanimously in favour—after all the Great North was Aberdeen's own railway—and so were a large number of merchants and others who proposed to send a deputation in support of the Bill. From further afield, too, came petitions in its favour. Edinburgh Town Council wanted it, so did the Edinburgh Chamber of Commerce and also the Convention of Royal Burghs. The Commercial Travellers' Associations of England and Scotland too were in its favour, and altogether 73 petitions were put in for it as compared with 49 against it—most of which came from places on the Highland system.

In support of their application the Great North argued that even with the train service they had got there had been an increase of seventy-eight per cent. in the number of passengers exchanged at Keith and Elgin between 1885 and 1894, and sixty-three per cent. in the goods traffic—though it took fourteen and three-quarter hours to get from Aberdeen to Inverness by the fastest goods train. Given a good service they were confident that there would be a great increase in traffic. Moreover, the existing train service was not only bad but badly arranged as well.   The Keith-Forres section was still looked upon by its owners as a feeder to their main line, and trains on it were arranged to suit the main line trains.   Consequently Great North trains had to be arranged to suit the timings of trains between Perth and Inverness—to the great inconvenience of everyone, but the Highland absolutely refused to run trains except to suit themselves.   By insisting on exchanging through traffic at Keith they were preventing a proper development of the Great North's line north of that point, which served a much more populous district than did the Highland between Keith and Elgin, and which therefore deserved and ought to be provided with a through service of trains to Inverness.   Nor was this all for they complained that the Highland trains were grossly unpunctual—a complaint which seems to have had little effect on the committee considering the Bill whose Chairman evidently considered that unpunctuality in Scotland was universal and no one had a right to expect anything else !   Lastly, they roundly accused the Highland of being generally obstructive and vexatious in a number of minor but very irritating ways.

To all this the Highland replied that if trains were unpunctual it was not their fault—they got them late from the South, and anyhow exact punctuality was impossible on a long single line like theirs.   It was no use for the Great North to expect to develop traffic—it was not there to be developed.   But if they did get running powers to Inverness and thereby diverted Highland traffic from the Highland Railway that Company would be too impoverished to provide proper service for its own system.   And if only the Great

North would give up their ridiculous system of working and look on the ends of their main line as what
they really were, namely branches, and run their trains
to suit the Highland's Mulben route, all would be
well!

The Committee listened to all this for many days
and in the end announced their finding as follows :—

"The Committee are unanimously of opinion that
the Highland Railway Company have placed undue
obstructions in the way of the development of traffic
and have shown disregard of the wants of the public
travelling between Inverness and Aberdeen. They
think that the action of the Highland Railway Company in regard to alteration of trains and to their
general dealings with the Great North of Scotland
have been vexatious, but in view of the unprece-
dented nature of the demand made, the want of any
reciprocal advantages, the absence of any sufficient
desire on the part of the community interested for
further competition, and in view of the demand
made and likely to be made on the Highland Company for the extension of their system, the Committee are unanimously of the opinion that the preamble of the Bill is not proved ; but they express
their earnest hope that all cause for complaint in
the future will be removed by the united action of
both companies by agreement if possible, or failing
that by the facility clauses of the Act of 1884."

This was a bitter disappointment to the Great North
but they lost no time in trying to carry out the hope
expressed by the Committee in the last sentence of
their finding.   At their instance a meeting of the

directors of the two Companies was held at Elgin in August of that year. The meeting seems to have been a friendly one but the negotiations come to nothing as the Highland still insisted on making Keith the point of exchange. The matter was then—at the Highland's instigation—referred to the Board of Trade, who appointed the Railway and Canal Commissioners as arbitrators and there for the moment it must be left.

While the two small Northern Companies were battling in the Committee Rooms of the House of Commons, their larger Southern neighbours were preparing to do battle in a much more spectacular and much less expensive way. It was a curious coincidence that twice the Great North should have chosen to make a frontal attack on the Highland in a year which was memorable in the annals of British Railway history for something very different—1890 was notable as the year in which the Forth Bridge was opened and 1895 will always be remembered as the year of the "Race to Aberdeen". Even now it is impossible to read the account of what happened on those August nights of 1895 without a thrill and inward regret that such things no longer occur. However wonderful an individual exploit may be—and wonderful some of them most certainly are—they lack the sporting element of a real "race" in which trains start from the same place at the same time and try to get to the same destination first!

When the racing trains started reaching Aberdeen about 6.30 a.m.—or earlier—the only Great North connection to the North was the slow 6.50 due in

Elgin at 10.25. But by the end of August these early arrivals had become settled and the Northern line accelerated their train beyond Keith to reach Elgin by Craigellachie at 9.54 and put on a new fast connection by the Coast line reaching Elgin two minutes later. In the following month a more drastic change was made. The old 6.50 was altered to leave an hour earlier and a new express was put on at 6.45, reaching Elgin by both routes at 9.15. This was the fastest train so far run between the two places, but it was nothing to what was to come. The Great North had evidently got a touch of the speed fever for in that autumn there were other accelerations as well, including the introduction of a new evening express leaving Elgin at 7.30 p.m. by the Coast and 7.32 by Craigellachie and reaching Aberdeen at 10.0.

Possibly from motives of what would now be called propaganda and possibly to bring to reality their dream of getting people from England to Inverness by their route in time to catch the North Mail, in August 1896 they suddenly drastically accelerated their 6.45 a.m. train. All stops south of Huntly were cut out as well as some along the Coast, and Elgin was reached at 8.48, 2 hours and 3 minutes from Aberdeen. For the run of $40\frac{3}{4}$ miles to Huntly only 45 minutes was allowed, that is an average speed of $54\frac{1}{3}$ miles an hour, which was a magnificent effort. Apart from the "Tourist" trains it must have been the fastest run in Scotland at that time. The timings over the rest of its course were also remarkably tight. Of course the load was light, usually seven six-wheelers weighing about 105 tons, but with those timings that was excusable!

As this was the fastest train ever run between Aberdeen and Elgin and as its timing was so far ahead of anything else ever attempted by a line of the size of the Great North, its timing is worth recording in full. That it was no paper promise is shown by the log of a run on November 6th, 1896, which appears in the second column. It is quoted from the late Rev. W. J. Scott's article in the "Railway Magazine", and unfortunately no other details are available.

			Schedule.	Nov. 6, 1896.
			a.m.	a.m.
—	Aberdeen	dep.	6.45	6.58
40¾	Huntly	arr.	7.30	7.42
	,,	dep.	7.35	7.47
			engine watered	
58¼	Tillynaught	arr.	7.57	8.6
	,,	dep.	7.58	—
61	Portsoy		8.4	8.12
66½	Cullen		8.13	8.21
72½	Buckie	arr.	8.23	8.29
		dep.	8.25	8.31
87¼	Elgin	arr.	8.48	8.49

40¾	Huntly	dep.	7.41
45¼	Rothiemay		7.49
48¾	Grange		7.56
53¼	Keith Junction	arr.	8.7
		dep.	8.10
54	Earlsmill (Keith Town)		8.12
64	Dufftown		8.28
68	Craigellachie		8.36
71	Rothes		8.42
80¾	Elgin	arr.	8.58

The Highland train left Keith at 8.20 and Elgin at 8.53 reaching Inverness at 10.15. Though there was thus a possible connection at Elgin they were unwilling to take on a through carriage as they maintained that through passengers should travel by Keith. The Great North refused to run a through carriage by that route and there was a first class row from which the passengers seemed to have suffered considerably! But either way the Great North at last had the satisfaction of giving passengers to the far North an opportunity of travelling by Aberdeen and yet catching the Mail from Inverness.

At this time also a special postal train was put on which left Aberdeen at 7.55 a.m. and calling at principal stations reached Elgin by the Coast at 10.34 and by Craigellachie at 10.33. It was a very light train consisting only of a Post Office sorting van, a brake van and a brake 3rd composite for the Coast, a van for the Craigellachie line and another van for Macduff. It continued to run till May 1897 when it was replaced by a new passenger and mail leaving Aberdeen at 8.5.

The very fast night trains from London were not destined to last long. One night in November 1896 the West Coast "Tourist" was derailed at Preston and that unfortunate accident ended high speed in Britain for many years. There was an alarm followed by hurried consultations between the railways concerned, the outcome of which was the slowing of the flyers by nearly an hour. From the point of view of speed development this was tragic, but it is doubtful if the travelling public really suffered much. It is hard to believe that anyone could have

J

wished to be hurled through the night at the highest
possible speed to be put out at Aberdeen—or anywhere else for that matter—at the uncomfortable hour
of half-past six in the morning. When, nearly forty
years later, Aberdeen was once again brought within
ten and a half hours of London it was by day—railways are more sensible now than they were in the
" 'nineties."*

The Great North kept their fast train running all
through that winter, but there was then another Parliamentary contest in view and they may have had
ulterior motives !

The decision of the Railway and Canal Commissioners was long in coming, and in the meantime the
relationship between the two Companies got no better.
So the Great North decided to make another application to Parliament for running powers between Elgin
and Inverness and presented a Bill for the session of
1897 which included a definite proposal for the doubling of the Highland's line from Elgin to Inverness.
But before the Bill had reached the Committee stage
the long-awaited judgment of the Commissioners was
announced.   Though it rejected the Great North's
plea as far as goods traffic was concerned, it gave them
all they asked for in regard to passenger traffic.
Elgin and Keith were each to become the point
of interchange for an equal number of trains,
through carriages were to be taken on from both

—* From the middle of July to the middle of August, 1896 there was also
another fast night service. A train left King's Cross at 10.0 p.m., and reached
Aberdeen at 8 30 a.m., while a corresponding train left Euston at 10.15 p.m.,
and arrived at Aberdeen at 8.50 a.m. It seems a pity that a service a some
such times as these was never tried again.

ELGIN STATION.

places, and at Elgin by both the Great North
routes if necessary. Each Company was also to
have the right to compel the other to run its connecting trains at the same average speed as its own.
The Commissioners remarked that they would no
doubt prepare a satisfactory time table, but as it was
not their job to do so but that of the Railway Managers, they told them to get on with it and submit their
proposals for approval.

This victory really cut the ground from under the
Great North's feet when they came to face the House
of Commons Committee. They were able, it is
true, to produce still further evidence of Highland
recalcitrance and they made what they could out
of the difficulties with which they were still faced
as far as goods were concerned as a result
of the Commissioners' judgment. For passengers
they urged that the service between Aberdeen
and Inverness should be as good as between
London and Aberdeen and promised to make it so
if they got their running powers. An overall time of
3 hours was suggested for express trains and even $2\frac{3}{4}$
hours was mentioned. They even promised to carry
out the doubling of the Highland line between Elgin
and Inverness entirely at their own expense. But all in
vain. The Committee had the Commissioners' decision
before them and the train service which resulted from
it which was really a very good one. Moreover, there
had been an important change in personalities since
the last fight. The Highland's old warrior, Mr.

Dougall, who had guided their destiny since their
birth, had died and had been succeeded by Mr. Steel,
who like Mr. Moffatt came from the North Eastern.
He was determined to do his best to improve the relationships between the two Companies, and though in
view of the long and bitter past it was hardly surprising that he could not at first imbue a similar spirit
into his opponents, or even all his subordinates—his
promise to work the new service loyally and effectively
must have weighed with the Committee. Anyhow,
they rejected the Bill and so ended the last engage-
ment of the war which had gone on for nearly forty
years.

The peace which followed was lasting because both
sides had something to show for their efforts. The
Highlanders had repelled the Aberdonians' attack on
their capital, but the latter had won an important tacti-
cal victory at Elgin, and though defeated in their main
objective they had no cause to feel disgraced. From
now onwards the relationship between the two old
antagonists became increasingly friendly and before
long there were even talks of a working agreement!

The travelling public, of course, benefited enormously by this peace. Unfortunately, at least one of
the Highland's contentions proved correct—there was
not a big increase of traffic to be got by such a
greatly improved service. But it was to take a few
years to discover this and until it was discovered the
North East corner of Scotland enjoyed what must

have been relatively the most ample service in Great
Britain.

The " Commissioners' Service " (as the new trains
were called) between Aberdeen and Inverness
came into operation on April 1st, 1897, but the
Great North's own service reached its zenith in the
following summer.   A new exchange platform known
as Cairnie Junction was opened on June 1st of
that year at the erstwhile Grange South Junction. It
was something of a phantom station for, being used
only for exchange purposes, its name did not appear
in the time tables, which must have been a cause of
much bewilderment to strangers. From now onwards
the practice of dividing down expresses at Huntly
ceased altogether and all express trains were either
divided or united at this new platform. It also made
possible some useful connections to and from Keith
and the Coast Line

The train service now provided was really a remarkably good one and the Great North, which only a comparatively few years before had been a by-word for
all that was bad, was now setting an example to many
much richer and more powerful concerns than themselves. Their expresses were composed largely of
electrically lit corridor stock, and for appearance,
comfort and smartness of working took a very high
place among the trains of that time. So good in fact
was the service that it is worth a full consideration
and a condensed time table of the main line and Inverness services is accordingly given.

Miles.			a.m.	a.m.	a.m.	a.m.	a.m.	a.m.	a.m.	p.m.	p.m.	p.m.	p.m.	p.m.
	Aberdeen	dep.	3.30	7.5	6.45	9.8	8.5	9.45	11.50	1.20	2.20	3.45	5.45	6.45
48	Cairnie Jn.	arr.			7.55		9.23	10.58		3.20	3.31		7.48	7.59
	Cairnie Jn.	dep.			7.59		9.27	11.2			3.37			8.5
53¼	Keith	arr.	5.15	9.8	8.13(†)		9.40(†)	11.15(†)	2.20		3.51(†)	5.19(‡)		8.21(†)
80½	Elgin via Craigellachie	arr.	8.40	9.0		10.18	12.5		3.40		4.40	6.50		9.5
	Keith H.R.	dep.	5.45	—		9.50	—		2.30			5.45		
108	Inverness' via Mulben H.R.	arr.	7.55		12.0				4.50			7.35		
	Cairnie Jn.	dep.	9.22				11.0	11.0			3.33	5.27(‡)		8.1
87¼	Elgin via Coast	arr.	8.57				12.5	12.5	2.10(‡)		4.40			9.5
	Elgin H.R.	dep.	9.0				12.15	12.15	3.47		4.50	7.10		9.15
123¼	Inverness H.R.	arr.	10.15				1.25	1.25	6.0		6.0	7.10		10.15

			a.m.	a.m.	a.m.	a.m.	a.m.	a.m.	p.m.	p.m.	p.m.	p.m.	p.m.	p.m.
	Inverness H.R.	dep.		6.30	7.0	9.20	10.32	10.55	1.40	2.48	3.10	3.50	6.0	7.26
	Elgin H.R.	arr.		8.22(‡)		10.22			2.40		5.5(‡)		7.16	
	Elgin via Coast	dep.		6.30		10.32	11.40	12.40(‡)	2.50				7.26	
	Cairnie Jn.	arr.				11.44			3.53				8.35	
	Elgin via Craigellachie	dep.		6.0	7.0		11.27(†)	11.40	2.48		3.50		7.26	
	Inverness via Mulben H.R.	dep.		8.15			12.0							
	Keith H.R.	arr.		8.25			12.10	12.55						
	Keith	dep.	6.15	8.34(‡)	8.35	11.48	10.10	12.55	3.37(†)	3.0	5.0	4.15	8.16(†)	5.0
	Cairnie Jn.	arr.				12.55	12.0		3.50	4.30	5.11(‡)	6.35	8.30	6.35
	Cairnie Jn.	dep.		9.55	10.55		12.10	1.5(‡)	3.55	4.40		6.45	8.38	6.45
	Aberdeen	arr.	8.30	9.55	10.55	2.0	2.0	3.0	5.10	6.5	7.10	8.50	10.0	8.50

† Earlsmill (Keith Town).
‡ Grange.

From this it will be seen that going North there were now four expresses from Aberdeen to Inverness by the Great North routes, of which the two 6.45's took three and a half hours, and the other two three hours and forty minutes. Through carriages were run on these by both Coast and Craigellachie routes. There was also the 8.5 a.m. which was an express as far as Elgin and slow from there, but without through carriages. Coming South the service was not so good as there were only two expresses and one semi-fast. This latter was the result of a compromise. When the Commissioners' service was being arranged Mr. Moffatt had wanted an up evening express leaving Inverness at 6.30 p.m. and reaching Aberdeen at 10.0, and Mr. Steel wanted the down 3.45 p.m. by Mulben to be an express. Neither side liked the other's suggestion and in the end Mr. Moffatt agreed to the up evening train being made a semi-fast on the condition that the 3.45 should be slow, and to this Mr. Steel also agreed.

The Mulben service consisted of four through trains each way daily. The down trains were little better than slow but one of the up trains—the 3 p.m.—was the fastest of any between the two towns taking only three hours and five minutes. Through carriages were run by all these trains.

The Great North's share of this service was more than creditable. Though the 6.45 a.m. was no longer run at the same very high speed as it had been in 1896-7 its time of two and a quarter hours to Elgin with nine booked stops and four conditional ones was remarkable. All the other down expresses and the

2.50 p.m. up took two hours and twenty minutes, and the up 10.32 only three minutes more. The traffic was not sufficient to allow any of the larger places to be passed and each of these trains had eight or nine booked stops and three or four conditionals. The down trains were without exception allowed five minutes at Huntly for the engine to take water and the up train stops included one at Schoolhill for ticket taking. The up 7.26 p.m. had a remarkably difficult timing, being allowed 2 hours and thirty-four minutes with no less than fourteen booked stops and eight conditional ones! All three fast trains ran through Keith Junction and called instead at Earlsmill, later known as Keith Town, as it was situated nearer the town itself. Their share of the Mulben service was also creditable as it included one fast down and two fast up trains between Aberdeen and Keith.

The best point to point timings were by the 6.45 a.m. down which ran from Dyce to Huntly, 34½ miles mostly uphill, in forty-five minutes with three conditional stops, and by the 10.32 a.m. up which ran from Huntly to a conditional stop (usually called) at Dyce in forty-two minutes.

The Coast line had also a sort of shuttle service. Trains started away in the morning from Elgin or Keith and returned home at night, working backwards and forwards between Tillynaught Junction and Buckie during the day. Altogether there were eleven down and ten up trains daily between these two latter places. There was also a train which ran right through from Elgin to Craigellachie to Tillynaught.

In addition to the above there were stopping trains

from Aberdeen to Inveramsay at 9.50 a.m. and 3.50 p.m., with through carriages for the Alford and Macduff lines and another to Inverurie at 7.5 p.m. This was the last train except on Saturdays, when it left at 7.45 p.m. and ran through to Macduff. On Saturdays also extra trains ran to Inveramsay at 3 p.m. and Inverurie at 10.40 p.m. There were, of course, corresponding up daily and Saturday locals.

The principal branch line trains had been by now considerably improved. Macduff had five trains each way daily and an extra one on Saturdays. The fastest of which took an hour and three-quarters down and ten minutes longer up, both connecting with main line expresses at Inveramsay. Alford had four trains daily and five on Saturdays, the best being the 3.50 p.m. down which took one hour twelve minutes, not at all bad for a purely stopping service which, of course, included the inevitable delay at the junction.

The Buchan line now had six down and five up trains serving Peterhead and Fraserburgh with one down and two up extra between Aberdeen and Ellon. The Cruden Bay branch had been opened the year before and an effort was being made to popularise it by running faster trains. Hence the afternoon train now left Aberdeen at 4.40 and running non-stop to Ellon in thirty minutes ($19\frac{1}{2}$ miles) reached Peterhead at 6.15 and Fraserburgh at 6.25. This was the fastest train of the day, but there were also two fast trains down in the morning. The up trains were not so good—the old 3.40 p.m. still being the best, taking one hour and forty minutes, but the evening train at 7.10 was only five minutes slower.

In the following year when most of the services were being reduced a further effort was made to popularise Cruden Bay. A new express was put on from Aberdeen at 10.10 a.m., reaching Ellon non-stop at 10.40, Cruden Bay at 11.6 and Boddam at 11.20. The up morning trains were re-arranged and a new fast service given from the branch leaving Boddam at 8.30 a.m., Cruden Bay 8.40, Ellon at 9.0 and reaching Aberdeen at 9.35. The 9.30 a.m. from Peterhead had all stops cut out between Ellon and Kittybrewster, this run being made in twenty-eight minutes, and Aberdeen reached at 11.14. In judging the speed of these non-stop runs it must be remembered that there was a severe check at Dyce Junction where the Buchan line leaves the main line and the Dyce-Ellon section is "the roof of a house" with very steep gradients on either side. Nothing, unfortunately, could make a success of the Cruden Bay line, and these efforts were shortlived.

By the summer of 1898 the Deeside service had also been improved. The up Deeside express now only took seventy minutes and the down seventy-five, and there were six other trains in each direction taking one hundred minutes down and rather more up on account of the fact that they called at several suburban stations.

The suburban services had also increased. Dyce now had fifteen down and sixteen up local trains which took twenty minutes each way with seven intermediate stops. Its total service was the very creditable one of thirty down and thirty-three up trains, the fastest

of which was allowed only nine minutes for the six
and a quarter miles.   On Deeside Culter now had
fifteen local trains each way with a total of twenty-
three each way.   Four down trains were non-stop and
took fourteen minutes, but the best up train took
twenty minutes.   The locals still took twenty-one
minutes down and twenty-two up, the latter including
tickets taking at Holburn Street.   As there were by
now eight intermediate stations in the seven and a
half miles between Aberdeen and Culter, this was very
smart work.   Moreover the suburban trains on both
the main and Deeside lines were composed of good
stock electrically lit, so no wonder they were popular!

All things considered—sparsity of population, difficult gradients and a high proportion of single line—
the Great North's train services of those days were
very hard to beat.   Moreover the smart timings of the
trains called for good station work and in this the
Great North were quite unbeaten. The average
length of stop at all but the most important places
was only about half a minute in the case of the main
line trains and must have been even less in the suburban ones.   This was one of the most praiseworthy
features of Great North working and it continued to
be a feature all the rest of its life.

The doubling of the main line had been extended
to Huntly by the end of 1896 and to Keith by 1898
except for the crossing of the Deveron at Avochie
which was not completed till two years later.   It had
been proposed to double the main line throughout to
Elgin by Craigellachie and at the same time to improve
the alignment of those parts of the Keith-Elgin section
where the curves were particularly sharp, but this

was not done so the doubling of the main lines never got beyond Keith. The doubling of the Deeside line was continued to Park in 1899.

All this progress was ill rewarded. The increase in traffics which had been so confidently expected did not materialise and there was a very severe slump in the whiskey business on which Strathspey so largely depended. On the other hand working expenses and interest charges were increasing so economy once again had to become the policy and in 1899 there began a pruning of the services which was continued more drastically in the following years. It was a sad end to a great endeavour.

We must now turn back a few years. Midway between the lower parts of the valleys of the Dee and Don there is a rich agricultural district which was not served by any railway. Various schemes had been proposed to remedy this state of affairs, but nothing came of them. In 1896 after the passing of the Light Railways Act two rival schemes were produced for a light railway between Aberdeen and Echt, one by the Great North of Scotland Railway and one by an independent syndicate. The Great North authorities had been giving a good deal of thought to light railway construction and had considered the idea of acquiring the Aberdeen tramways with a view to working them in connection with a system of light railways serving the district round Aberdeen, of which the Skene and Echt line would have been one.

As originally proposed this line would have started at the West end of the city and would have been connected down town there with the main line by a railway down to Kittybrewster, but this part of the scheme looked so expensive that it was abandoned. The proposal finally put before the Light Railway Commissioners was for a junction between the light railway and the Aberdeen tramway system with running powers over enough of the latter to enable connections to be made with the main railway system. The Town Council of Aberdeen strongly opposed this idea and it had to be dropped, despite the railway's promise that the engines should consume their own smoke, and that even the goods trucks should not be offensive. The rest of the scheme for a light railway thirteen and a half miles long from Oldmill to Echt, passing round the loch of Skene, was authorised, the rival project having been withdrawn. The railway was to have been built and equipped on the most approved lines embracing the best features of the Bavarian and Saxon light railways and also some of those of the Belgian and Dutch.

Owing to the failure to get permission to join up with the tramway system this railway was left completely in the air at the Aberdeen end, so the original idea was revised and powers were obtained to make a light railway from Oldmill to Kittybrewster. The continuation of this line down to a junction with the Deeside line, thus making a circular line round the West of Aberdeen, was also considered but given up owing to its costliness.

This railway was never made. The three miles from Kittybrewster to Oldmill which included a tunnel would have been very expensive in any case, and when it came to the point the Town Council's requirements as to bridges and so on were found to make it even more so. Some of the landowners, too, proved unwilling to give their land free and, as the cost of making the line was considerably increased by these two things, it was abandoned and the powers obtained for making it allowed to lapse.

CHAPTER SEVEN.

THE TWENTIETH CENTURY.

BY the end of the nineteenth century the Great North system was practically complete. Only one short branch from Fraserburgh to St. Combs was made after that and it was opened on July 1, 1903. It was a light railway five and a half miles long serving the fishing villages of Inverallochy and St. Combs. Arrangements for making two more light railways had, however, reached an advanced stage when the War came. In 1908 a syndicate was formed to promote a light railway from Fraserburgh along the coast to Rosehearty and then inland to New Aberdour —a total distance of nine miles. This scheme had got the promise of a grant from the Treasury and its promoters had also come to an arrangement with the Great North of Scotland Railway, but there it stayed. The other proposed light railway would have joined Maud Junction on the Buchan line with Turriff on the Macduff line. It was promoted in 1914 by the Light Railways and Development Syndicate Limited of Aberdeen. This line, which would have been 21½ miles long, and would have served a prosperous agricultural district, received the blessing of the Treasury, Light Railway Commissioners and the Board of Agriculture for Scotland (as the Department of Agriculture for Scotland was then called) and negotiations with the Development Commissioners for a grant of public money had been successfully completed when further progress was stopped by the War.

The provision of double line had also been practically completed by the opening of the new bridge over the Deveron at Avochie on April 30th, 1900, which completed the doubling of the main line to Keith. Only one other short section was doubled after that, and from Park to Elrick signal box on the Buchan line many years later.

There was, however, considerable progress in other directions. By the beginning of the century the new works at Inverurie were beginning to take shape. Building had commenced in 1898 and in 1901 the carriage department was moved in. The locomotive department followed a year later and in 1903 the office staff arrived. The last to come was the Permanent Way Department, which came in 1905. The works covered an area of twenty-four acres and consisted of five blocks of shops in addition to the Locomotive Superintendent's block of offices. They were built of granite from the Tyrebagger Quarries and were so designed that it would be possible to enlarge them without difficulty—another instance of the Great North's optimism of the " 'nineties "! The lay out was admirably designed to facilitate their work. Most of the machinery was new, but some of the best at Kittybrewster was moved over. Mr. Pickersgill was a great believer in electricity and it was extensively used for power in the works.

The population of Inverurie was increased by

Suburban Train near Kittybrewster.

Train at St. Combs Station.

twelve hundred people by the coming of these works and the Railway Company built houses for the new population. In addition to a house for the Locomotive Superintendent there were four blocks of houses with gardens for the office staff and foremen and five blocks of three-roomed and two blocks of four-roomed houses for the workmen. All these houses were lit by electricity. There was also a good deal of ground made available for garden plots and a large Park. A hall and rooms for recreation were also built. Technical classes were arranged in the winter evenings for the engineers and apprentices, and the social side was encouraged by the formation of dramatic and musical societies. There was also an ambulance society. A new town had come into being at the North end of the old town—possibly the latter benefitted, but it was an expensive luxury for the railway shareholders.

The old station at Inverurie was at the south end of the town but with the coming of the works a new station was built about half a mile further north and near the works. It was an admirable example of what a station should be, having ample offices and long, wide and high platforms very adequately sheltered by verandah roofs. The up platform was an island the outer side of which was used by the Old Meldrum branch trains. The engine which worked these got the name of Meldrum Meg, but it seems to have been applied to each one in turn and not to have belonged to any one in particular—there was only ever one at work on the branch at one time.

The Great North did a good deal of station rebuilding in the late 'nineties and early years of the present

K

century and it was all very well done.   The most important station to be rebuilt was Elgin, which was
completed in 1902.   For some years previously there
had been much talk of a joint station with the Highland.   Negotiations went on but in the end the Highland decided that their own station was good enough
for their requirements and therefore they did not feel
justified in spending money on a new one.   The Great
North consequently had to go on by themselves and
they built a very good station indeed.   There was one
long platform which connected with the neighbouring Highland station and was used by the through
trains, and three bays, one each for the Coast, Craigellachie and Lossiemouth trains.   There were good
buildings and a spacious circulating area, which was
well protected by an ample roof as were the platforms.
Station rebuilding was not limited to the main line
and some of the best examples of new stations were
to be seen on the principal branches.   Nor was the
modernization limited to the larger places for many
of the smaller stations were improved as well and
adequate platforms were a feature of most of them.
Of course there were exceptions but on the whole by
the end of its life the Great North's stations were
decidedly good.

In the spring of 1904 Deeside had its first experience of a form of locomotion which in course of time
was to transform all local transport.   In May of that
year the Railway Company started a service of motor
omnibuses between Ballater and Braemar.   Five services were run each way daily in connection with the
trains to and from Aberdeen.   The time taken to

Braemar from Ballater was an hour and twenty-five minutes—not fast according to modern ideas but a considerable advance on the old horse coaches which had taken two and a quarter hours. The early buses ran on solid tyres and these gave some trouble at first but this was soon remedied. Though there was a good deal of opposition to begin with from the owners of the coaches and others who liked the old-fashioned way of travelling the service quickly became popular and it was the pioneer of a large number of similar services run by the railway from all parts of its system.

To regularise what they had done and prepare the way to future developments in 1905 the railway obtained a Provisional Order under the Private Legislation Procedure (Scotland) Act 1899 which gave them the widest possible powers to work road motor transport. During the next few years rapid progress was made in this enterprise and by the spring of 1907 they had seven services in regular operation as well as the summer only "Three Rivers Tours".

The first of these, which came in 1905, was a service between Huntly and Aberchirder which was the first to serve a purely agricultural district. The distance between these places was eleven and three-quarter miles and the time taken was seventy minutes. Two buses were run each way daily and a third on Saturdays. 1906 saw a large increase, services being provided between Alford and Strathdon, Undy Station on the Buchan line and Tarves and Methlick, Aberdeen and Cluny and Culter on the Deeside line and Echt and Midmar, but this last service was soon changed to run from Aberdeen. Between Aberdeen and Cluny and Aberdeen and Midmar there was a choice of routes and a rather complicated service was run to take full advantage of this. The Strathdon service, which was largely a tourist one, consisted of two buses each way daily in summer and one in winter, while on the Udny-Tarves route two daily services were run all the year round—also using alternative routes. This service, however, was not a success and was soon withdrawn. In the spring of 1907 a service of two buses each way daily and another on Saturdays was put on between Aberdeen and Newburgh 15 miles away on the Aberdeenshire Coast.

All the services centering on Aberdeen started from Schoolhill Station and in later years a special refreshment room was opened there for the convenience of passengers using them. A feature common to them all was that an extra service was worked from Aberdeen on Fridays to suit people who had come in for the markets held on that day.

The Three Rivers Tours which were started in June 1907 were a great effort to increase tourist travel. They linked the three valleys of Dee, Don and Spey and provided a variety of possible routes. A motor charabanc was run between Ballater and Strathdon connecting at Dinnet with the Deeside trains and at Strathdon with a motor bus from Alford which continued to Cock Bridge almost at the head of the Don Valley. From here to Tomintoul the road was too steep for motor buses and that part of the journey had to be made by coach. Tomintoul was connected by a regular summer motor bus service with Ballindalloch on the Strathspey line. The various connections were so arranged that tourists had a choice of several alternatives—they could either visit all the valleys or any two of them. Though these tours continued to run till the War and were revived again after it, they were never so popular as they deserved to be for they served a very beautiful part of Scotland.

The last service to be instituted was from Fraserburgh to Rosehearty and New Aberdour. This came in November 1912 and was given the most frequent service of any route. Two down services were run from Fraserburgh to New Aberdour and three up ones, the balancing mileage being made by an extra service from Rosehearty to New Aberdour. In addition to this there were six services both ways between Fraserburgh and Rosehearty.

By 1914 the railway had a fleet of thirty-five passenger road vehicles, a total which was reduced by one by 1922. They were mostly single decker buses but two of them had seats outside for ten passengers. For the tourist routes there were five charabancs, two seating twenty-eight people and three seating eighteen. These vehicles were of different makes, but all were worked well within their capacity as the schedules were very easy. All had solid tyres.

In addition to these passenger vehicles the railway also owned fourteen goods wagons, the stock consisting of eight Foden and three Clayton five-ton lorries each adapted to haul a three ton trailer and three old bus chassis converted into lorries for parcel and goods work. They worked on three regular routes—Aberdeen to Newburgh, Alford to Strathdon and Ballin-

dalloch to Tomintoul, but they were also used anywhere if there was a demand for them.

The total route mileage worked by all these services
was one hundred and fifty-nine.   They were not a
very paying proposition in the pre-war days.   Speaking at the Annual General meeting in February, 1914,
the Chairman said that the total receipts for the previous year had been £10,702 and the expenses including depreciation, £9,958, leaving a profit of only
£744—not a large return on the £34,000 capital
which had been invested in them.   However, they fed
the railway and so benefited the Company as a whole
and were undoubtedly a great convenience to the
localities they served.

In 1904 Mr. William Ferguson died.   He had been
a director of the railway for thirty-seven years and
Chairman for twenty-five.   The story of his reign has
been told.   At the time he became chairman it would
have been a brave man who would have predicted the
amazing change which came over the railway under
his guidance.   The travelling public and the Company's shareholders alike had good reason to be grateful to him and those who so ably helped him in
this work.   He was succeeded by Sir David Stewart
who had twice been Lord Provost of Aberdeen and
was one of that City's leading business men.   He was
also a son of the Mr. Stewart who had been vice-
chairman of the Railway in the early 'sixties, so his
family had had a long connection with it.

The relationship between the two northern railways
had by now become cordial and in 1905 there was a
proposal to amalgamate them.   Five years previously

there had been an attempt to come to a working agreement but it came to nothing. Under the scheme now put forward the amalgamated Company was to be called the "Highland and North of Scotland Railway" and was to have its headquarters in Aberdeen. A Bill was promoted for the session of 1906. The proposal was duly approved by the Great North shareholders, and an actual majority of those Highland shareholders who voted was also in favour of the scheme. But the opposition there was strong and a very large number did not vote at all. In these circumstances the Highland Directors did not feel that they could go on and with the consent of the Great North Board the Bill was withdrawn.

There can be no doubt that the amalgamation would have benefited both the Companies and the public and its defeat was very regrettable. Though not strictly speaking competitors, the two systems met at a number of places and the North of Scotland would certainly have been served more efficiently and economically by one Company than by two. But it was not to be, for the scheme was never revived and when Parliament decided to combine the railways into four groups the Highland was put in the London, Midland and Scottish and the Great North of Scotland in the London and North Eastern. No one is likely now to question the wisdom of the policy of grouping, but it is at least questionable whether the best possible arrangements were always made. In the immediate post-war years our statesmen were in a great hurry and no doubt the quickest way to get a workable scheme was to amalgamate railways whole, but it might have been a wiser policy in the long run to have gone more slowly for by so doing many of the anomalies of the present arrangement might have been avoided—this amongst others.

Though the amalgamation failed, the idea of a closer working agreement remained to take practical shape two years later. In the spring of 1908 an arrangement was come to whereby the principal trains between Aberdeen and Inverness were worked by one engine throughout. In order that each company's engine should start from their own sheds in the morning the Highland engines had to work over the Great North routes from Elgin to Aberdeen and the Great North's engines over the Highland route from Keith to Inverness. The Highland engines worked the 9.8 a.m. and 1.40 p.m. from Inverness to Aberdeen by the Coast Line, returning with the 2.20 p.m. via Craigellachie and the 6.45 p.m. via the Coast, while the Great North engines worked the 3.30 and 10.5 a.m. trains from Aberdeen to Inverness, returning with the 11.5 a.m. and 3.20 p.m. trains from Inverness to Aberdeen. To balance the mileage fairly they also worked the purely Highland trains from Keith to Inverness at 1.55 p.m. and from Elgin to Keith at 3 p.m. The engine which worked the 1.55 down returned to Keith by the 6 p.m. from Inverness, which it worked by the Coast line as far as Cairnie Junction. The curious result of this arrangement was that all the best Great North expresses were worked throughout by the engines of their erstwhile enemy !

When this arrangement first started the Highland used their "Small Ben" class locomotives to work these trains but with the coming of the "Bigger Bens" in

the following year one of them was put to work the
afternoon turn. This arrangement did not last very
long for in 1911 they were withdrawn and the Great
North took over the working of these trains themselves, but the Highland "Small Bens" continued to
work the morning turn. The whole arrangement
ended with the War and was not reintroduced after it.

Both Companies' choice of engines had been
limited owing to the fact that they used different
brakes—the Great North having adopted the Westing-
house and the Highland the vacuum.

Mr. Moffatt resigned in 1906. Mr. A. G. Reid who,
as Passenger Superintendent, had done so much to
help him build up the improved train services, had left
some years previously to become the General Manager
of the Dublin, Wicklow and Western Railway, and had
been succeeded by Mr. William Deacher so now none
of the Big Three who had transformed the old Great
North remained. Mr. Moffatt had been Secretary as
well as General Manager, but on his retirement the
offices were divided, Mr. George Davidson, the Company's Solicitor, becoming General Manager and Mr.
T. S. Macintosh the Secretary—positions which they
filled till the end of the Company's life.

In 1899 and the early years of the present century
there was a general reduction in the train services
which affected most parts of the system. On the main
line the number of down expresses was reduced to four
in summer and three in winter and these (except the
6.45 p.m. in summer) served one route only. The two
fastest took two hours and twenty minutes but owing

to the cancellation of some of the slow trains the others had extra stops added and took longer in consequence. All four had through carriages to Inverness, the best service being given by the 6.45 p.m. which still took three and a half hours. Coming up there were still three services by the Great North routes but the morning one had been slowed and now left Inverness at 9.8 a.m. and Elgin at 10.22, the arrival time at Aberdeen still being 12.55 p.m. By the Mulben route there were three services in each direction with through carriages. The up fast train no longer ran so the fastest train by this route was now the 10.10 a.m. down which took three hours and fifty minutes, the average time being about five minutes longer. It did not, however, retain its supremacy long as by the time the through engine workings were introduced it had been slowed at both ends. These trains also had connections to the Coast or Craigellachie lines or to both of them and in addition there were other local trains serving the different parts of the main line so the service, though no longer lavish, was fully adequate. During the last years before the war there were some further slowings of which the most serious was the addition of ten minutes to the time of the up mail which left Elgin at 2.40 p.m., the Inverness connection leaving there at 1.25.

There was, however, a spirited attempt to improve the services on the principal branches in the summer of 1906. The most important alterations were on the Buchan line and they included the acceleration of the down morning train to reach Peterhead in ninety minutes and Fraserburgh in ninety-five. The evening down train which had been one of the sufferers from the economies of the previous six years, was again quickened, while an up morning express was instituted in ninety-five minutes from Peterhead and one hundred and three from Fraserburgh. A fast Saturday train was also put on to Cruden Bay in just over an hour. The morning alterations, however, proved unpopular and the old service was restored in the autumn of that year, but a fast evening service in both directions in summer continued to run till the War. An attempt to improve the mid-day connections from the Deeside line to the South fared no better, but an alteration of the up morning service from Alford which brought that town within an hour of Aberdeen remained. Mixed trains had been reintroduced on the Macduff line during the economy period but from 1906 passenger and goods trains were again separated during the summer months.

An interesting development took place on the Deeside line in 1914. An attempt was then made to develop the outer-suburban service between Aberdeen and Banchory by running a somewhat fuller service. An arrangement had also been come to with the late Sir Thomas Burnett by which the express trains were allowed to pass Crathes station without stopping. This opened the way to a drastic acceleration of the down train which was altered to run to Ballater in the very smart time of sixty-five minutes, calling only at Torphins and Aboyne and slipping coaches at Banchory. Slip coaches were never widely used in Scotland and this was the only instance of their use on any Scottish line except the Caledonian. The timing of thirty-three minutes to Torphins (twenty-three and three-quarter miles) was very good considering the gradients. The up train called additionally at Banchory to pick up the carriages slipped off the down train the evening before, and so took one minute longer for the whole journey. Unfortunately this interesting experiment was cut short by the War and was never tried again.

The Deeside service reached its maximum in that year with seven daily trains each way to and from Ballater and four extra ones to and from Banchory. These included the up and down expresses and the 5.50 p.m. up was also "fast" from Banchory. In addition on Wednesdays and Saturdays an excursion train was run to and from Ballater, the down train being non-stop to Torphins and taking eighty-five minutes for the whole journey with three intermediate stops. There were also two extra trains between Aberdeen and Banchory on those days and late evening trains on Saturdays as well. The suburban service between Aberdeen and Culter consisted of eighteen trains each way daily and Culter's service consisted of twenty-eight trains each way daily and three more on Saturdays. Two goods trains were also run each way between Aberdeen and Ballater daily.

Powers to double the Deeside line to Banchory had been obtained at the end of last century, and some preliminary steps to carry this out were made at this time. There was also a renewed demand in certain quarters for a continuation of the line to Braemar coupled with the construction of a road through Glenfeshie to connect Braemar with Kingussie. As will be seen later both these schemes were recommended by the Committee which was appointed at the end of the War to consider local transport in Scotland. The railway is unlikely ever to be made, but the road is a geographical necessity, as by linking up with the road from Kingussie to Fort William it would give direct communication from East to West across Scotland at its broadest part and make unnecessary the great detour either North or South which through travellers now have to make.

Great efforts were made to encourage excursion traffic from 1905 till the War. Not that excursion trains were a novelty on the Great North. A Saturday excursion to Deeside had been started as far back as 1881, which in that year took ninety-five minutes to reach Ballater and ran altogether seven times. By the end of the century it had become a regular Saturday excursion. But Aberdeen has two half-holidays —Wednesdays and Saturdays, some people observing one and some the other for there is no suggestion that everyone in Aberdeen had two half holidays a week! To meet this excursions now began to run on both Wednesdays and Saturdays. The most notable of these was the Strathspey excursion which began running in June 1905. At first this train ran non-stop to Craigellachie, sixty-eight miles in eighty-five minutes —a remarkable speed for an excursion train over such a hilly road—but after a few years a stop was inserted at Dufftown, sixty-four miles from Aberdeen, which were run in eighty-one minutes. The time taken to Boat of Garten (one hundred and one and a quarter miles) was two and a half hours, the up train taking two minutes longer, so the average speed for the double journey was just over forty miles an hour— very good going over a hilly road with many sharp

curves, and nearly half of which was single line. For
one year the train was run through on the Highland
line to Kingussie, but this proved unpopular locally
so was not repeated.   Later on arrangements were
made for cold luncheons to be served but they had
to be ordered in advance for they had to be prepared
before leaving as there were no arrangements for
cooking on the train. The Company took great pride
in this train which always included saloon and corridor carriages in its make up, and the greatest efforts
were made to run it punctually.   And for all this the
return fare was half-a-crown!

It is interesting to compare this with an early
Strathspey excursion which was run in connection
with the Aberdeen autumn holiday in 1882. This train
left Aberdeen at 8.20 a.m. and after calling at some
suburban stations was due at Grantown, where it
stopped at "about noon".   Coming back it left Grantown at 4.45 p.m., and calling at Ballindalloch and
Aberlour as well as the suburban stations, reached
Aberdeen "about 8 p.m."   The first class return fare
was 6/- and the third class 3/-.

A few years after the introduction of the Strathspey train another fast excursion was put on by
the Coast line to Elgin.   Though not quite so good
as the Strathspey train its speed was more than creditable. A non-stop run was made to Tillynaught Junction at about forty-seven miles an hour and Elgin was
reached with five more stops along the Coast in two
hours and ten minutes at an average speed of just over
forty miles an hour—a good deal faster than the best
ordinary train.   The up trains took five minutes
longer.

Mention has already been made of the Deeside excursion and a motor coach trip was now run up the valley from Ballater as far as Balmoral in connection with it. In addition to these long distance excursion trains there was also a series of short distance ones from Aberdeen to Cruden Bay, to the Alford Valley line, to Inverurie and to Banchory every Wednesday and Saturday.

Aberdeen, however, was not the only place whose interests were considered, for every town of any size had special cheap fares arranged for its own weekly half-holiday. In addition to this there was a very comprehensive system of cheap day and half day fares on the Strathspey line, and from there to Lossie-mouth. An interesting example of co-operation with the Highland was the granting of special cheap fares from Aviemore to Tomintoul by rail to Ballindalloch and by motor bus from there. It will be seen, there-fore, that the Company's efforts to encourage excur-sion travel were very comprehensive, and they proved increasingly popular up till the War.

By the end of last century the traffic at Aberdeen had quite outgrown the capacity of the old Aberdeen joint station—indeed, as far back as the 'eighties there had been complaints of the inadequacy of that sta-tion, and in 1883 the Great North had prepared plans for a new one. Nothing was done then, but during the later 'nineties there were prolonged discussions between the two owning Companies as to how matters should be improved. The Great North were anxious for a complete rebuilding of the whole place including the widening of the approach from

Ferryhill Junction but the Caledonian were not at first prepared to go so far. However an agreement was eventually concluded and in 1899 an Act known as the Aberdeen Joint Station Act was obtained, which gave powers to rebuilt it at a cost of two hundred thousand pounds. Needless to say, this sum was greatly exceeded before the work was finally completed.

It was a long time before there were any obvious signs of the re-building for which powers had thus been obtained. To make room for the enlargement of the passenger station it was necessary to shift the goods stations further to the east, and there was a dispute with the Harbour Commissioners about the exits from these goods stations, from which tracks were to be laid to the docks. Moreover there was a great deal of heavy preliminary work which had to be done which, though very costly, was not obvious to the general public. There was in consequence a good deal of grumbling at the apparent delay.

That people should have grumbled was not surprising for the condition of the old station was really a disgrace. No alterations had been made to the south end since it was built, and the accommodation there provided was hopelessly inadequate for the traffic requirements—the platforms consisting only of the south end of the long through platform and two bays. The usual arrangement was that the Caledonian trains used the main platform, the Great North of Scotland's Deeside trains the bay next to it, while the North British trains, which only got there by virtue of running powers from Kinnaber Junction, were pushed away to the outside bay, the platform

INTERIOR OF THE OLD ABERDEEN JOINT STATION, LOOKING NORTH.

CIRCULATING AREA OF THE NEW ABERDEEN JOINT STATION, LOOKING NORTH.

of which was not only narrow and low, like all the others, but the end of it was on a sharp curve. The super-elevation of the rails which was consequently necessary raised the level of the carriage doors to a most uncomfortable height above the platform, and how ladies who affected the hobble skirts which were so fashionable about the end of the Edwardian period ever got into a North British train at all will ever remain a mystery!

To make matters worse there was a bottle neck outside the station, as there was only a double line of running rails from Denburn Junction to Ferryhill over which had to be worked not only all the passenger and goods trains of the Caledonian, North British and Deeside lines, but also all the two former companies' light engines going to and from their sheds, which were—and still are—out beyond Ferryhill.

At the north end the Great North were rather better off. The long main platform had been lengthened to provide a covered way to the Palace Hotel. The outside platform of the old bay had been extended by a wooden platform to a sufficient length to allow of another bay being made on its far side, but this wooden addition was quite outside the main station and entirely devoid of any protection whatever.

The old offices and the circulating area were also quite inadequate for the needs of the traffic, and the roof leaked badly in many places. There were times, too, when the station was almost dangerous. All the fish traffic was at that time worked through the passenger station, and the platforms were frequently covered with fish slime which on a wet day made them

L

extremely slippery. It was a remarkable thing that no legs were broken by passengers climbing from the trains on to the low platforms.

With such an inadequate station very serious delays to traffic were inevitable, and the wonder is not that delays were serious, but that the traffic at busy times was ever got through the station at all.

The first improvement was the widening of the approach from Ferryhill by the Caledonian Railway. This was expensive work, as the line there is carried along a viaduct, but the widening was essential if any improvement was to be made in the movement of traffic. The first obvious improvement in the station itself came in 1907, when a start was made with new through platforms on its west side. These were intended primarily for suburban traffic but were also used for excursions. Prior to that, suburban trains had to use any platform available, which was a great inconvenience to passengers, who never knew from where they were going to start. The new platforms were brought into use in 1908, and the following year a new Entrance and Booking Office with the necessary waiting rooms was built at the corner of Guild Street and Bridge Street, which gave much easier access to them.

It was, however, some time yet before the principal buildings could be tackled, but when this work was once commenced it was carried through very rapidly. As the Great North were the principal owners this work was entrusted to their Engineer, Mr. Parker.

The foundations of the new station were commenced on May 28th, 1913, and by the end of July,

1914, all the new platforms were in use. The masonry work was completed by the end of August of that year, and the last remnant of the old station disappeared in October following. It cannot be said that its disappearance was the cause of any regret! Owing to the War a certain amount of work had to be postponed so the new station was not finally completed till after the end of the War.

Externally the new station has no particular architectural merit; internally, however, it is spacious and well planned. As in the old station the main block of buildings is on its east side. The central feature is a spacious Booking Hall from which there are two exits leading directly onto the Circulating Area. The main block also contains the refreshment and waiting rooms, hairdressing room, lavatories and other offices such as cloakrooms and a bath room. On the side of the Circulating Area opposite the entrances from the Booking Hall and facing them is a block of buildings which includes the station master's office, telegraph office and bookstall. Above the latter is a particularly clear train indicator in which the names of the stations are written in letters large enough to be read comfortably all over the Circulating Area. This block of buildings is flanked on either side by flights of stairs which lead to a bridge giving access to the western platforms. The whole effect of this is very pleasing and is one of the main features of the station. Another interesting feature, though not so obvious, is the provision of heating pipes to each platform by means of which trains can be heated before starting.

There are altogether four through platforms, the most westerly one of which is a short one which was intended for suburban work, but others are of full length. In addition, there are five bays at the south end and four at the north, leading directly off the circulating area, so there is ample platform accommodation. The total length of the platforms of the new station is 11,340 feet as compared with 4,247 in the old, the longest platform being the main through one which has a length of 1,596 feet.

The circulating area is entirely covered by a roof, but this does not extend over the platforms, each of which is protected by its own "umbrella" roof. The protection thus afforded is fully adequate, and by leaving the running lines unroofed the station can be kept much cleaner, as smoke and steam from the engines goes straight into the outer air.

The signal cabin, which controls the north end of the station, has 105 levers, and was the largest on the Great North system—that at Inverurie with 69 levers coming next.

Including sums which the two Railways had to spend outside the station in connection with the modernisation of the Caledonian at Craiginches and the Great North at Kittybrewster and the rebuilding of the goods stations, the total estimated cost was about £800,000.   The late Lord Banbury, who was for many years Chairman of the Great Northern Railway, is said to have remarked on one occasion : "There is no money in stations". This may be so, but the reverse is certainly true—bad and inadequate stations are not only expensive to work but have an adverse effect on receipts. Despite its great cost, the new station was therefore probably not only a necessity but also in the long run a sound investment for its owning Companies.

CHAPTER EIGHT.

ROYAL JOURNEYS.

THE Great North of Scotland Railway's claim to be a Royal line dates from their absorption of the Deeside Railway, but that Company was a Royal Route from its earliest days.

The first Royal Journey was made on October 13th, 1853, when Queen Victoria and the Prince Consort were leaving Balmoral for London. The Royal Party left Balmoral at 8.30 a.m. and drove to Banchory, which was then the terminus of the line. Though the day was fine there had been much rain previously, and the drive down the valley took twenty-five minutes longer than had been expected owing to the slippery state of the road. The old Banchory station was rather further east than the present one and here great preparations had been made. A triumphal arch with a crown in the centre had been erected at the station entrance and the platform was covered with crimson cloth. The Queen was received on the platform by Mr. James Innes of Raemoir and the chairman and directors of the Deeside Railway, and a great crowd had assembled to see the departure of the royal party. The royal train left at 12.15 p.m. and reached Ferryhill, which was then still the terminus of the Aberdeen and Deeside Railways, at 1.43, the fifteen and a half

G.N. OF S.R. ROYAL TRAIN.

miles having thus taken twenty-eight minutes. As the Deeside Railway owned no engines at that time the royal engine must have been provided by the Aberdeen Railway whose rolling stock was then used for working it.

At Ferryhill the Queen was met by the civic authorities of Aberdeen and the two Sheriffs. After a short stop the journey was continued to Edinburgh, luncheon being taken at Stonehaven, where a special stop was made for the purpose, and this became the usual practice in the early journeys from Balmoral. Edinburgh was reached at 6 o'clock, of course by Perth and Larbert. In those days the Queen and the Prince Consort used the East Coast route for their journeys to and from Scotland.

Three days previously to this there had been another interesting journey over the new line when Queen Victoria's mother, the Duchess of Kent, had used it when leaving Balmoral. Her journey took half an hour, having commenced at 1.15 and finished at 1.45.

Banchory continued to be the arrival and starting point for the royal trains for the next seven years, but with the opening of the extension to Aboyne the royal journeys were extended to that station too, the new line being used for the first time in 1860. The Queen had attended a Review of Volunteers in Edinburgh on the previous day so the first journey to Aboyne began at Edinburgh, which was left at 9 a.m. Perth was reached at 11.10, Bridge of Dun at 12.38, and Ferryhill at 1.55. The journey up Deeside was started five minutes later and Aboyne was reached at 3.10. In the account of the journey which appeared in the "Aberdeen Journal" at the time the first part of the journey was described as "fast", but the second part as slow—which is not surprising considering the heavy gradients and sharp curves on that part of the line. Aboyne station was decorated with heather and the Second Company of Kincardineshire Volunteers was drawn up on the platform inside the station. Outside was the regular guard—a company of the 93rd Highlanders. Luncheon was served to the royal party in the station rooms which "contained four suites partly designed for such occasions".

After the Prince Consort's death the Queen went to Balmoral twice a year—once in the spring and once in the autumn, the first spring journey being made in April 1862. The journey was now made to and from Windsor, the journey being made over the Great Western and West Coast Railways. This route was always used thereafter with rare exceptions—such as when the Queen opened the ill-fated first Tay Bridge.

Though the Queen's privacy was very rigidly guarded in England greater latitude in this respect was allowed North of the Border, and at Aberdeen particularly was this the case. Though the Deeside Railway's Terminus had gone with that of the Scottish North Eastern from Ferryhill to Guild Street in 1854, the former remained the point of exchange for the Royal Train. Here it was met by the Lord Provost and magistrates and other dignitaries of the City of Aberdeen. It was a very awkward place as it was only a junction with no station and consequently no platform, so they all had to wait on the rail level. But their ladies and friends were able to get a better position on an adjoining cattle ramp! An enclosure was erected to which entrance was by ticket only, but there was always a large crowd outside and the royal presence evoked great scenes of loyalty. The Queen always made a point of showing herself at the window and bowing her acknowledgements to the greetings of the assembled people. After a few years two pairs of portable steps were provided for the convenience of people getting in and out of the train, for there were generally telegrams or messages to be taken to the Queen. While this was going on the Deeside Railway engines came on to what had been the back of the train, which now became the front for the rest of the journey. From Ferryhill Junction to Aboyne the 30¾ miles took about an hour including a stop for water at Banchory.

Ballater Station was first used in 1867. In those days and for many years after it was a small and awkward place consisting of little more than a booking office and one platform which was hardly long enough to accommodate the royal train. Until 1893 the points were worked by hand and it was only in July of that year that a signal box was built. Considerable further improvements were made in 1896 when a roof was provided for part of the platform and a porch at the entrance to the station which had then become a much more adequate place. Later a refreshment room was added and the station is the same now as it was in the later Great North days—except, of course, for the London and North Eastern Railway's name board.

From the time it was first used till the end of the reign Ballater station was the scene of at least

least two royal arrivals and departures every year.
and the procedure became standardised. Queen
Victoria disliked high speed and no attempt was ever
made in her time to make any great acceleration of
her train—at least as far as the Deeside line was concerned, so the journey down Deeside at the end of
the century took about an hour and a quarter. The
train at that time consisted of the Queen's royal saloon,
which had twelve wheels, four eight-wheeled saloons,
four six-wheeled coaches and three six-wheeled vans.

Queen Victoria's journeys on the Great North were
not entirely confined to the Deeside line, for she made
three others over the main line between Aberdeen and
Keith. The first of these was made on September 6th,
1872, when she went from Balmoral to visit the Duke
of Sutherland at Dunrobin. The train consisted of
two brake vans, "a truck for Her Majesty's Fourgon",
five carriages and a "single and double royal saloon".
Drawn by two engines it left Ballater at 10.20 a.m. and
reached Aberdeen at 11.30—three minutes early.
Aberdeen Station had been specially decorated for the
occasion, and according to the press report it had
"rather an elegant appearance". The decorations
consisted of "a centre pillar with real floral decorations from which were strings of flags stretching to
both sides of the Station". During the stop there of
ten minutes the Lord Provost presented the Queen
with an address from the City and several people were
also presented to her. Between Aberdeen and Keith
the train slowed down as it passed the stations so that
the people could get a better view of the Queen. Keith,
where a great crowd was waiting, was reached at 1.30
—five minutes late, and here the train was handed

West Coast Royal Train on Deeside Line.

Ballater Station.

over to the Highland Railway. Elgin was reached at
1.58, where there was a stop of five minutes to allow
the Provost to present an address. Passing Forres
and Nairn the train slowed down, the next stop being
Inverness which was reached on time. Ten thousand
people had collected to give the Queen a welcome to
the Highland Capital and needless to say another address was presented to her by the Provost—and this
happened again at Dingwall. The journey ended at
Golspie at 6 o'clock, and the Queen drove from there
to Dunrobin.

The return journey was made by night, starting
from the Duke's private station at Dunrobin at 11.30
p.m. There were, of course, no ceremonies on this
occasion, the only stops on Highland territory being
at Dingwall for water and Elgin. The Great North
took the train over at Keith, which was left at 4.25
a.m., Aberdeen was reached about 6.30 and Ballater
at 8 o'clock precisely.

Almost exactly twelve months later the Queen went
from Balmoral to Inverlochy, on the West Coast. The
outward journey was made by way of Perth and the
Highland main line with a long drive from Kingussie.
A different route was selected for the return—this time
by way of the Caledonian Canal and Inverness. For
the Canal part "Messrs. Hutchinson's Saloon Steamer
'Gondolier'" was used. A drive of some six miles was
involved from Dochgarroch to Inverness, where a
special train was waiting. This left at 3.45 p.m. and
reached Keith at 5.30, after short stops at Forres and
Elgin. Once again a great crowd assembled here including the local volunteer corps, whose band played

the "National Anthem". There was no other ceremony and Aberdeen was reached nine minutes early
at 7.10, the leading engine being driven by Mr. Cowan,
the locomotive superintendent. For the last part of
the journey the officials of the Deeside Line took
charge ; Aberdeen was left at 7.24 and Ballater
reached at 8.45. It is recorded that the Queen looked
tired at the end of this journey, and no wonder !

King Edward VII went only once a year to Balmoral—in the autumn. Owing to the fact that he
made several journeys apart from those to and from
the South, and also that his journeys frequently did
not coincide with those of Queen Alexandra, there
were nearly as many royal journeys a year on the Deeside Line as in Queen Victoria's reign.

His first journey to Scotland after his accession was
made on the night of Friday, 27th—Saturday, 28th
September, 1901. The West Coast route continued
to be used and the Royal Train left Euston at 9.15
p.m. Stops were made at Whitmore (where the
engines were changed) at 12.15 to 12.22 a.m., Carlisle 3.40 to 3.47 and Perth at 7.11 to 7.18. Aberdeen
was reached at 9.15. Here breakfast was taken in the
Palace Hotel, the journey up Deeside being continued
at ten o'clock and Ballater reached at 11.15. This was
the only occasion in that reign on which the Royal
Train used the Joint Station at Aberdeen on its journeys to or from the South—on all others Ferryhill continued to be its stopping place.

In the following year the King made the longest
journey on the Great North of Scotland Railway ever
undertaken by a reigning sovereign. After his ill-

ness and the fatigues of the Coronation he decided to
go North in the Royal Yacht by way of the West and
North Coasts. After paying a visit to the Duke of
Sutherland at Dunrobin he finally landed at Invergordon on September 8th and the journey from there
to Ballater was made by train. The Duke of Sutherland lent his own private saloon for the use of the
King and Queen, and the Great North royal saloon
was used by the equerries and suite. For the rest the
train consisted of two composite carriages and two
brake vans. The Highland Railway sent a pilot
engine—the "Duke"—twenty minutes in advance of
the Royal Train, but the Great North stuck to their
custom of doing without one.

The Royal Train left Invergordon punctually at
11.20 and reached Elgin at 1.10. There had been
some doubt as to whether the train should use the
Highland line to Keith or be transferred to the Great
North at Elgin but the latter course had finally been
chosen, so the Royal Train and its pilot used the Great
North's station at Elgin. From there it was sent by
the Coast line, the time allowed for the eighty-seven
and a quarter miles journey from Aberdeen being two
hours and five minutes. Two Great North engines
replaced the one Highlander which had brought the
train so far, but the five minutes allowed in Elgin were
slightly overstayed so the train was three minutes late
in starting. That, however, was made up and Aberdeen was reached sharp on time at 3.20 p.m. After
changing engines the train left again at 3.25 and Ballater was reached at the appointed time of 4.30, having made almost the longest possible through journey
on the Great North of Scotland's system.

During this reign the Great North was twice called on to provide a complete Royal Train of their own. The first of these occasions was in September 1903, when they had the honour of being commanded to provide the train for the King's journey from Rufford Abbey, where he had been staying for Doncaster Races, to Balmoral. The train sent for this purpose consisted of two eight-wheeled brake vans, two eight-wheeled composite coaches, a six-wheeled first class corridor coach, a six-wheeled saloon and the royal saloon—known by its owners as "Saloon No. 3". The journey was made by day from Ollerton on the then Lancashire, Derbyshire and East Coast Railway, and the East Coast route was followed. It had originally been intended that the train should stop at Ferryhill, but at the last moment it was decided to bring it into the Joint Station. From Edinburgh to Aberdeen it was allowed three hours and ten minutes with a stop at Dundee, and it arrived a minute or so before its booked time of 5 o'clock. The Lord Provost and magistrates of the City and the railway officials were waiting on the platform, but everyone else was excluded. During the train's short stay the Lord Provost was introduced to the King. Ballater was reached at 6.10, the journey from Aberdeen having taken an hour and five minutes—which had become the usual allowance for royal specials on the Deeside line and remained so for the rest of the reign.

The second occasion on which the Great North had to supply a royal train was when the King, accompanied by the Queen, went from Balmoral to Aberdeen to open the Marischal College at the time of the Quater-Centenary anniversary of Aberdeen Univer-

sity in 1906. The make-up of the train for this journey was almost the same as for the journey from Ollerton three years before, but without the first-class
coach. Only one engine was used and it was gaily
decorated for the occasion, a thing which was, of
course, never done for the usual royal journeys. A
special Time Table of the journey, showing the arrival
and departure times and passing times of the principal stations was prepared for the royal party. It
was printed in purple with the Royal Arms in gold at
the top. For the inward journey in the morning Holburn Street Station was the terminus, and a roof was
built over the "up" platform there for the occasion.
Though luckily it was not needed as the day was
gloriously fine, a generation of passengers and ticket
collectors must subsequently have blessed that royal
journey for all up Deeside trains stopped regularly at
Holburn Street for ticket examination, and a good
many people used to leave the train there. The
journey of 42 miles took exactly an hour. The return
journey in the afternoon was made from the Joint
Station—the journey home taking the usual sixty-five
minutes.

The London and North Western Railway had built
two very fine new royal saloons in 1903 and as King
Edward VII always travelled by the West Coast route
if travelling to or from London, they were soon well-
known on Deeside   His journeys to London were
usually made by day, leaving Ballater about nine in
the morning and taking about twelve hours on the
way.   Stops were usually made at Ferryhill, Perth,
Carlisle and Crewe, but on one occasion—in 1903—
the run from Carlisle to London was made non-stop.

Queen Alexandra, however, frequently used the East Coast route on her journeys to and from Wolferton or London and Ballater.   The Great Northern and North Eastern Railways built two new royal coaches in 1908 and they were fairly frequent visitors to Deeside from then till the War.   But the West Coast was, and has always remained, the usual route for the royal journeys.

On his last three visits to Scotland King Edward went first to Speyside and the journey was made up the Highland line from Perth to Boat of Garten. The Great North took charge there for the eighteen mile run to Advie—for which only twenty-five minutes were allowed—smart work.   In 1907 and 1908 the journey from Speyside to Balmoral was made by motor-car, but on the last occasion the King went from Speyside to the West Coast, and the journey from Ballater was made from Kentallen on the Caledonian Railway's Connel Ferry to Ballachulish line.

King Edward VII's last journey from Balmoral was made on October 11th, 1909. He travelled by day as was his wont when going South, and left Ballater at 9.20 a.m., arriving at Ferryhill at 10.23. After stops at Perth 12.16—12.29, Carlisle 3.40—3.45 and Crewe 6.45—6.50, Euston was reached at 10 p.m. His reign had been a notable one for the Great North. During those nine years thirty-one royal trains for the King and Queen were run over the Deeside line. No other reigning sovereign travelled over so much of their system as he did, for no other monarch were they called on to provide a train and neither before nor after that period were their royal trains so fast as they were then. The reign of King Edward VII can be looked

upon as the height of the Great North's achievements
in the matter of royal travel.

During the reign of King George V the time allowed
for the royal journey up and down Deeside was gradually extended. At the end of the reign it was, in fact,
a good deal longer than at the end of Queen Victoria's,
but the train had increased in weight vastly in the
intervening years. At the end of her reign it weighed
about 250 tons, but by forty years later it had increased to 480 tons. As far as the Great North was
concerned, King George V's reign produced no very
notable Royal Journeys. The last one for which they
were responsible took place on October 9th, 1922.
Two years before the old system of stopping the train
at Ferryhill had been abandoned, so this journey was
made right into the Joint Station at Aberdeen. Ballater was left at 5.30 p.m. for King George always
travelled south by night, and Aberdeen was reached
at 6.55 p.m. So ended a chapter in Royal Travel.

Our own royalty were not the only ones to travel
on the old Great North of Scotland, for on several
occasions it was used by reigning sovereigns of other
countries. In the summer of 1889 the Shah of Persia
made a short private visit to Deeside. His arrival co-
incided with the Aberdeen summer holiday and great
crowds of people came to see him. As usual Ferryhill
was the place of exchange from the Caledonian—by
which he had travelled from Buchanan Castle—to the
Great North, and here he was met by the City Magistrates, headed by the Lord Provost, who presented
him with an address. For their accommodation a
special platform, covered with a crimson cloth, had
been erected opposite where the royal saloon was ex-

M

pected to stop. There was also an enclosure to which
some of the public were admitted by ticket, as in the
case of the Queen's journeys   A guard of honour was
provided by the First Volunteer Battalion of the
Gordon Highlanders. The train arrived at Ferryhill
soon after four o'clock and left at 4.10, reaching Ballater at 5.30. Here the station and town were gaily
decorated to receive the Shah and special festivities
were arranged in his honour by his host, Mr. Mac-
kenzie (as he then was) of Glenmuick. After staying
a night there he went to Invercauld where he was the
guest of Sir Algernon Borthwick (afterwards Lord
Glenesk). Invercauld is some fifteen miles from Ballater and on his return journey the time taken for the
drive down was misjudged and he arrived forty
minutes before his train was due to start. This caused
a great deal of perturbation as nothing was ready, and
the guard of honour had not arrived ! However, they
duly arrived at their proper time and were inspected
by the Shah before he left at 12.30.   Ferryhill was
reached at 2.9, but as the time of its arrival was not
generally known only a few people were there. The
Lord Provost, however, was present and gave him a
basket of Aberdeen strawberries to refresh him on his
journey South !

Seven years later their Imperial Majesties the
Czar and Czarina of Russia paid a private
visit to Queen Victoria at Balmoral. They
landed at Leith on September 22nd, 1896, in
dreadful weather which followed them all the
way to Aberdeen and ruined the decorations there
which had been put up in their honour. This was a
pity, for considerable preparations had been made to

receive them. A special platform was erected at Ferryhill by workmen specially brought from Perth. Work was only commenced on the morning of the Imperial arrival, and it was completed only just in time! A high wooden hoarding gave the people on the platform some protection, but also hid the view of what was going on from everybody else.

The Royal Train left Leith at 2.30 p.m. A stop was made at Dundee where an address was presented by the Lord Provost and tea was brought to the Royal Saloon. Aberdeen was reached at 5.34—two minutes early. Here also the Lord Provost presented an address and Miss Ferguson, the daughter of the Chairman of the Great North Railway, presented a bouquet to the Empress. To enable this to be done a gangway was put from the platform over the "up" line of rails to the Royal Saloon. While this was happening the North British engines which had brought the train so far were taken off and two Great North engines attached to the other end. Ballater was reached three minutes early at 6.57. Here also most elaborate preparations had been made. The station was decorated in black and yellow—the Imperial colours—and in the passage from the platform to the entrance mirrors were hung. Electric light was installed in the station and also in the station square and along the road to Balmoral as far as the Burgh boundary. This was provided by a plant specially installed, steam for which came from an engine standing in the south bay of the station. Their Imperial Majesties were received with great enthusiasm not only in Ballater but all along the road to Balmoral, which was reached at 8.5.

The day before their arrival the Queen had paid a visit to Ballater station to inspect the arrangements made there and expressed herself thoroughly satisfied with everything.

The visit lasted until October 3rd when they left for Portsmouth to rejoin their yacht "Standart". They do not seem to have had the same gift of punctuality that has always characterised our own Royal Family for their train was eleven minutes late, leaving Ballater at 11.11 p.m.   It consisted of sixteen carriages and there were said to have been ten tons of luggage.   Ferry-hill was reached at 12.22½ a.m. and here the Caledonian Railway took charge.   They ran a pilot engine —No. 36—and the train was hauled by two of the celebrated "Dunalastair" Class, Nos. 723 and 734, then quite new, but there is no record of the Great North machines.   All the lost time and more had been recovered by Perth, which was reached at 2.26 a.m. The journey was continued by way of Oxford where there was a stop from 2 to 3 p.m. next day for lunch, and the train finally arrived at Portsmouth at 5.23 p.m.

In August 1906 the King and Queen of Spain paid a private visit to Lord Leith of Fyvie at Fyvie Castle. They travelled on the night of August 12th-13th from Southampton, leaving there at 9.50 p.m.   The journey was made by the West Coast route which was reached by way of Addison Road and Willesden Junction. Aberdeen was reached at 11.30 next morning and the journey to Fyvie Station on the Macduff Branch was started at 11.37 and took fifty-three minutes—the distance being thirty-one and a quarter miles. Fyvie Station being a somewhat simple place, a special temporary awning was put up for the Royal visitors.   After a stay of four days they left again in the early morning of August 17th after taking part in a Ball given in their honour. The special train left at 2 a.m. and got to Aberdeen fifty-five minutes later en route for Crieff, which was reached at 9 o'clock next morning, three hours having been spent at Methven to fill up time.

Two other Kings also used the Great North, the King of the Belgians who went at least twice to Balmoral, and the King of Portugal, but no special trains were run for these as they were travelling "incognito".

Lastly, in 1913 the Dowager Empress of Russia accompanied Queen Alexandra on a visit to Balmoral. They travelled from Wolferton, the journey up Deeside taking an hour and twelve minutes. The return journey was made by night to London leaving Ballater at 10 p.m. and arriving at Ferryhill at 11.10, the West Coast route being used from there.

So it will be seen that a very large proportion of the Great North of Scotland Railway's line was used by Royalty at one time or another. The most elaborate arrangements were made for these journeys and every possible precaution was taken for the safety of the Royal travellers. During the time of the Fenian outrages considerable alarm was felt for the Queen's safety when travelling to and from Balmoral. To make certain that nothing untoward occurred men were posted within sight of each other along the whole route from Windsor to Ballater, and this precaution was continued by the Great North until the end of its days. Most railways ran a pilot engine fifteen or twenty minutes ahead of the Royal Special but this was not done by the Great North who trusted to their other arrangements. These were elaborate enough. On the single part of the line no train was allowed for at least twenty minutes before the Royal Train was due to pass. On the double line all trains meeting it had to slow up to ten miles an hour. Each section had to be cleared for the train fifteen minutes before it was due and no one except the station staff was allowed on the platform of any station while it was passing. All facing points had to be clipped and padlocked twenty minutes before the train reached them, and all level crossing gates (of which there were many) also locked till it had passed.

For the benefit of the passengers the London and North Western Railway used to produce a very elaborate timetable. On the outside was a picture of the train in colour and also a diagram of it. Inside was a timetable giving the arrival, departure and passing times of all stations en route and also a gradient profile of the whole journey. The county in which each station was situated was also shown. The passengers thus had a very complete idea of how they were getting on.

The Great North did not detail any engines particularly for Royal Trains. Their habit was to select two which were being repainted that year and give them perhaps a little extra finish. Anyhow, those that were employed were always beautifully kept and added not a little to the fine appearance of the train.

CHAPTER NINE.

ROLLING STOCK.

THE first Locomotive Superintendent of the Great North of Scotland Railway was Mr. D. K. Clark, the well-known writer on locomotives. It appears that he did most of the work from his London office making occasional visits to Aberdeen and leaving the actual supervision on the spot to his assistant, Mr. Ruthven. His term of office was neither long nor happy as there were constant disagreements between him and the directors.

The first engines to be built for the Railway were from his design and were twelve in number—seven passenger and five goods. As delivered they were all of the 2-4-0 type but apparently the goods engines had originally been designed as six-coupled engines. They had 808 square feet of heating surface and cylinders 15 in. in diameter with a stroke of 20 in. The coupled wheels of the passenger engines were 5 ft. 6 in. diam. and those of the goods engines 5 ft., both having 3 ft. 6 in. leading wheels. Their weight in working order was $23\frac{1}{4}$ tons. The passenger engines were numbered 1 to 7 and the goods engines 8 to 12. They were built by Messrs. W. Fairbairn of Manchester, the passenger engines having cost £2,250 and the goods engines £2,200. They were all ordered for delivery by the expected opening date, but deliveries were very late

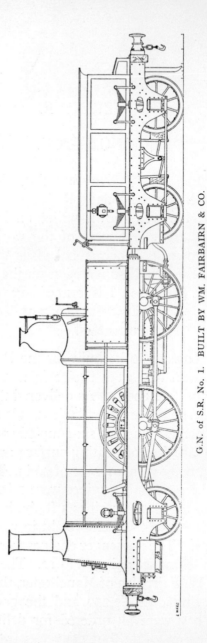

G.N. of S.R. No. 1. BUILT BY WM. FAIRBAIRN & CO.

G.N. of S.R. LOCOMOTIVE No. 4.

Photo : F. Moore.

and the first goods engine did not arrive till June, 1855.

These and all subsequent Great North engines for many years were fitted with Mr. Clark's patent smoke preventing system which was also said to result in considerable fuel economy. It consisted of a series of holes in the sides of the firebox above the fuel for the admission of air through which jets of steam were projected which circulated the air in the firebox.

Owing to the shortage of engines those which had been delivered were hardworked at first—doing as much as 160 miles a day. Two of them broke down, so, as that only left five engines to do all the work, they must have been kept moving!

Mr. Clark resigned in July 1855, and was succeeded by Mr. Ruthven, the Works Manager, whose salary was fixed at the princely sum of £160 a year. Banking engines were required at this time for working the Harbour branch which was opened in 1856 as part of the main line and tenders for two tank engines were called for. Messrs. Beyer, Peacock got the order on

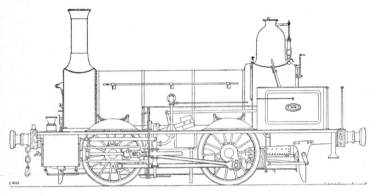

0-4-0 BANKING ENGINE DESIGNED BY MR. CLARK AND
BUILT BY BEYER PEACOCK & CO. IN 1856.

an estimate of £1,950 for each engine. They were 0-4-0's weighing 25 tons with 4 ft. 6 in. wheels and 15 in. by 24 in. cylinders. Their tanks were between the frames and under the boilers. They were destined to have a very long life, and were in fact the longest lived of any Great North engines as they worked on that system till 1916 when they were sold to the Government for war work. They were re-boilered in 1887 by Mr. Manson and during the latter part of their life they were used for shunting at Keith and Elgin, and also at the Daluaine distillery. They retained copper capped chimneys and brass domes till the end of their life though after re-boilering the domes were placed in the centre of the boiler. As originally built they were over the firebox, as was the case with all the early Great North engines ; they were numbered 13 and 14.

In July 1856 three more passenger engines similar to Nos. 1—7 were ordered from Messrs. Fairbairn at a cost of £2,200 each. A further engine was also ordered from them for £2,100 for delivery in July 1857. These four engines were numbered 15—18.

Mr. W. Cowan became locomotive superintendent in 1857 and the last of the 2-4-0's were from his designs. They came from Messrs. Stephenson & Co., Nos. 19-24 in 1860 and Nos. 25-27 in 1861, and were goods engines similar to Nos. 8-12, except that they had 16 in. by 20 in. cylinders. With this class started the habit of building classes the number of whose engines consisted of three or a multiple thereof. With one single exception this rule was not departed from for thirty-five years !

Mr. Cowan's next engines, which were also built by

By courtesy of Major S. A. Forbes.

G.N. OF S.R. LOCOMOTIVE No. 22 AS REBUILT.

Messrs. R. Stephenson & Co. were the Great North's first 4-4-0's, and they were very nearly the first engines of that wheel arrangement in this country. As originally built they had bogies with outside springs, but these were replaced later by more normal ones. Their coupled wheels were 5 ft. 1 in. in diameter.   Their boilers which had a diameter of 3 ft. 9¾ in. had 161 tubes 11 ft. 4½ in. long with a diameter of 1⅞ in., giving a heating surface of 898.2 sq. ft., to which must

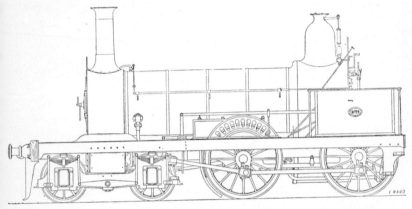

G.N. of S.R. No. 28. BUILT BY ROBERT STEPHENSON & CO. IN 1862.

be added 67.4 sq. ft. provided by the firebox, making a total heating surface of 965.6 sq. ft.   The grate area was 10.25 sq. ft. and the working pressure 140 lb. per sq. in.   The two outside cylinders were 16 in. in diameter and had a stroke of 22 in.   In working order the engines weighed 34 tons 10 cwt. and the four-wheeled tenders 15 tons 10 cwt., making a total of 50 tons.   The wheel base of the engines was 19 ft. 6¾ in. and of the tenders 8 ft. 6 in.; total wheel base being 35 ft. 0¾ in., and length over buffers 43 ft. 8¼ in.

Nine of these engines were built and they were delivered as follows :—

28—30   ... in 1862.
31—34   ... in 1863.
35 & 36 ... in 1864.

They were built to work in the Strathspey district and in all probability it was the sharp curves which abounded there that suggested bogies instead of rigid leading wheels.

On September 13th, 1878, No. 31 burst her boiler. She was working the 3 p.m. train from Craigellachie to Boat of Garten and at the time of the explosion was standing in Nethybridge station. A cleaner who was on the footplate was knocked unconscious by a piece of flying metal, but otherwise no one was seriously injured. These engines had seams along the bottoms of their boilers and it was grooving along this seam which caused the accident. The Board of Trade inspector considered that the last test of the boiler had been insufficient, as it was only tested to 170 lb. per square inch with cold water and the working pressure was then fixed at 140 lb.—a test up to 200 lb. for a working pressure of 120 lb. would have been normal, he considered.

After this, No. 31 was off duty for nearly eighteen months, being given a new boiler in January, 1880, and the other engines were all similarly fitted by March, 1883, Nos. 28 and 30 being the last to be so treated. New bogies of a more modern type were fitted at the same time. but otherwise they retained their early appearance—except for the addition of a cab—and continued to do so all their lives. They were the last engines to be at work in that form. The first to be broken up were Nos. 29 and 31, which went

G.N. OF S.R. LOCOMOTIVE No. 33 AS REBUILT.

By courtesy of Major S. A. Forbes.

in 1905. No. 36 went in 1910, Nos. 28 and 33 in 1913, Nos. 30 and 32 in 1917, and Nos. 34 and 35 in 1920, these latter having been on the duplicate list since 1915 and 1914 respectively. All that then survived had had their boiler pressure reduced to 120 lb. per square inch in 1907.

Once having adopted the 4-4-0 wheel arrangement the Great North never again departed from it for tender engines. In this way they were unique and in another respect also they must have been almost if not quite unique—they never had any single wheelers. Not that single wheelers would have been very suitable for their requirements, but unsuitability does not seem to have prevented their use on other systems! Considering how extremely popular this type was during the nineteenth century, it is rather remarkable that it never found favour on the Great North.

As has already been told, the Great North took over the rolling stock of the Morayshire and Banffshire Railways in 1863, the former Company's engines being given the numbers 41 and 42 in the Great North list, the latter Company's 37-40. No. 39 was broken up almost at once and this number went later on to a Deeside engine. The history of these engines has already been told in Chapter Two, so need not be repeated here.

In 1866 six new engines, larger and more powerful than the "28" class, came from Messrs. Neilson & Co. of Glasgow. They had a more modern type of bogie and were the earliest or almost the earliest bogie engines to have lateral play. They had 5 ft. 6½ in. coupled wheels, 16 in. by 24 in. cylinders and a working pressure of 140 lb. per square inch.   The wheel base of the engine was 20 ft. 5 in., and of the tender 8 ft. 6 in., the total being 36 ft. 5⅝ inches.   These engines weighed 36 tons and the tenders 15 tons 5 cwt. The original tenders had four wheels, but some of these engines were later given larger ones with six wheels.   All of them were rebuilt by Mr. Manson and Mr. Johnson between November 1889 and February 1891.—Their copper capped chimneys were retained and brass covered domes, but these latter were placed in the middle of the boiler.   In this form they ran for many years and for length of life rivalled Nos. 13 and 14.   Nos. 43 and 46 were the first to be scrapped, going in July 1921.   No. 47 followed in the next month, but the other three passed on to the London and North Eastern Railway after the amalgamation of 1923.   No. 45 was the last to go to the scrap heap in 1925, having previously in that year hauled a train of old Great North coaches in the Railway Centenary procession at Darlington.   As originally built they were known as Class "B" and after rebuilding as Class "K".

After 1866 there came the long period of forced economy and the only addition to the Companies' locomotive stock for the next ten years were the engines taken over from the Deeside line when it began to be worked by the Great North in 1867. These engines, which have already been described, were given the numbers 39, 40 and 49-53.

It is a curious fact that it was the earliest engines of all the three small companies taken over by the Great North which was the last to be scrapped. Thus

G.N. OF S.R. LOCOMOTIVE NO. 47, CLASS "K," AS ORIGINALLY BUILT.

G.N. of S.R. Locomotive No. 45, Class "K" with train of old coaches at the Railway Centenary, Darlington, 1925

By Courtesy of L.N.E.R.

Deeside No. 2, built in 1854, which became G.N.S. 39, lasted till 1883—three years longer than Deeside No. 8 built in 1866. "Banffshire" Nos. 1 and 2 lasted even longer—till 1885 but they were only built in 1859, while "Morayshire" No. 3 was also built and scrapped in the same years. The earliest Morayshire engines, however, were never taken over. All the Deeside engines did not last so long. No. 4 (G.N.S. 49) was scrapped in 1875 and Nos. 5, 6 and 7 (G.N.S. 50, 51 and 52) went in 1876, 1878 and 1877 respectively.

Partly to replace these Deeside engines and partly to provide a necessary increase of stock, six larger and more powerful engines were built to Mr. Cowan's designs by Messrs. Neilson & Co. in 1876. They had the same sized coupled wheels as the "43" Class, 5 ft. 6½ in., but their cylinders were larger—17 in. by 24 in., and they also had larger boilers and fire-boxes, the heating surfaces of which were 1,023.4 sq. ft. and 84 sq. ft. respectively. The grate area was 14 sq. ft. and the working pressure 150 lb. per square inch. They had six wheeled tenders with outside springs above the frames and with a carrying capacity of 3¼ tons of coal and 1,950 gallons of water. The engine wheel base was 20 ft. 6 in. and that of the tender 11 ft. 0 in., the total wheel base being 39 ft. 0½ in. In working order they weighed 41 tons 3 cwt., and their tenders 28 tons, making a total weight of 69 tons 3 cwt. They were given the numbers 49, 50 and 54-57, but No. 57 subsequently had her number changed to 52, her original number being given to one of the next type.

These engines came from the same builders two

years later. They had similar boilers and fire boxes to the last lot but their coupled wheels were 5 ft. 7 in. in diameter and their cylinders 17½ in. by 26 in. They had a slightly longer wheel base and were rather heavier, 42 tons 4 cwt. as compared with 41 tons 3 cwt. They differed considerably in outward appearance from all previous Great North engines as the splashers over the trailing wheels were rounded and not square and in consequence the shape of the cab was also different. The tenders, too, were larger and more modern looking having their springs hidden. They carried 3¼ tons of coal and 1,950 gallons of water and weighed 29 tons, so the total weight in working order of these engines and tenders was 71 tons 4 cwt. They were numbered 40, 51, 53 and 57-62 and were known as Class "M".

Mr. Cowan's last type, known as Class "C", came in the following year, 1879, and consisted of three engines Nos. 1, 2 and 3, being thus the first to replace any of the Great North's own stock. They were generally similar to the two previous types but had 6 ft. 1 in. coupled wheels, the largest so far fitted to any engines on the Great North. Their wheelbase was slightly shorter than that of the "M" Class and they were also slightly lighter than those engines.

The last twelve engines were strikingly handsome machines. They had the usual characteristics of the early Great North engines—outside cylinders, a large brass dome with inverted bell mouth tops set on the firebox, and copper capped chimneys. The fireboxes were higher than the boilers and deep brass bands covered the joining of them and also that of the boiler

G.N. OF S.R. LOCOMOTIVE NO. 57 (SUBSEQUENTLY 52), CLASS "L."

By courtesy of the North British Locomotive Co. Ltd.

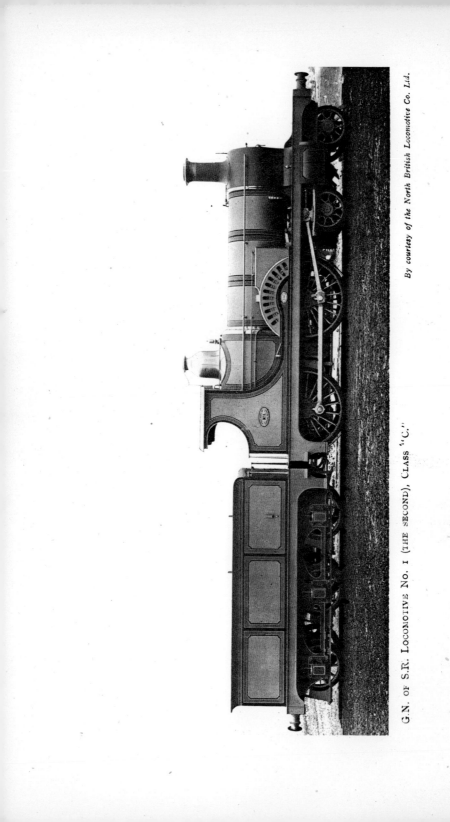

G.N. of S.R. Locomotive No. 1 (the second), Class "C."

and smoke box, and indeed they had a lavish display
of brass all over them. Cleaning was not so expensive in those days ! Altogether they had the appearance of being strongly built and their design had very
clean lines so they avoided the almost ramshackle
appearance of many of their contemporaries.

These last three types were rebuilt by Mr. Pickersgill
in the latter years of the 19th and early years of the
20th century. They retained their old wheel and cylinder dimensions, but had new boilers and fireboxes.
The heating surface of the boilers, which were 11 feet
long and had a mean diameter of 4 ft. 5 in., was
1,018.5 sq. ft. and of the fireboxes 100 sq. ft., total
1,118.5 sq. ft   The grate area was 15.64 sq. ft. and the
steam pressure 150 lb. per sq. inch. The new boilers
had standard mountings—chimney, dome and enclosed Ramsbottom safety valves, which gave the
engines a thoroughly modern appearance. All the
types differed slightly in weight as rebuilt, the "L"
class weighing 41 tons 3 cwt. and their tenders 28
tons, the "M" class 42 tons 4 cwt. with 29 ton
tenders, and the "C" class 42 tons with 29 ton tenders.
The first to be rebuilt was No. 40 in October 1896
and the last No. 2 in October 1904. (No. 52,
rebuilt in 1897, differed from the rest, having been
given a square cab with side windows.) In their new
form they did much useful work on branch line and
lighter main line work. The Macduff and Strathspey
sections were perhaps their happiest hunting grounds,
but they were to be found at one time or another all
over the system—except on the smallest branches.
They were all passed on to the London and North
Eastern but were scrapped soon afterwards. All but

N

No. 40 had gone by the end of 1927 but she lasted another five years and was not broken up till June 1932.

These engines were the last of an epoch in Great North locomotive history, for though Mr. Cowan remained locomotive superintendent for some years after they appeared he built no more engines and his successor Mr. James Manson, who came from the Glasgow and South Western, completely revolutionised the design for the engines on his new line. All the old fashioned features, brass domes, copper capped chimneys, open splashers and so on, were swept away. Inside cylinders now became the standard and the only Great North engines built after this with outside cylinders were four small tanks for working the traffic of Aberdeen Harbour.

Mr. Manson's first tender engines were, however, smaller than Mr. Cowan's later ones. They had 6 ft. coupled wheels with 17½ in. by 26 in. cylinders. The total heating surface was 1,036 sq. ft., the steam pressure was 140 lb. per sq. inch. They weighed 37 tons 2 cwt. in working order. Six of them were built by Messrs. Kitson & Co. of Leeds in 1884, and they were known as Class "A" and numbered 63-88. No. 68 was the engine in the accident at Brucklay in September 1889. When working a mixed train from Fraserburgh she was turned into the goods yard at that station by mistake and crashed into the bank at the end of it killing a man who was standing near looking after a cart. Three more engines generally the same as these but with 5 ft. 6 in. coupled wheels came from the same makers in the

G.N. OF S.R. LOCOMOTIVE No. 3, CLASS "C," AS REBUILT.

By courtesy of Major S. A. Forbes.

following year. They were known as Class "G" and numbered 69-71. The Great North engines were divided into First, Second and Third class engines and both these types were ranked as Second class. For some not very obvious reason the " G " Class engines were allowed to work between Aboyne and Ballater in the latter 'eighties and early 'nineties when otherwise all but Third class engines were forbidden to do so. As their weight was the same as that of the "A" Class it is not easy to understand why only these "G" Class machines were allowed to do so.

Mr. Manson had found a very ancient and miscellaneous assortment of tank engines, only two of which had actually been built for the Great North, the others having been taken over from the Deeside, Morayshire and Banffshire Railways as has already been seen. He at once set about to provide the railway with some new ones and Messrs. Kitson & Co. built six from his designs in 1884 and three more in the following year. They had six coupled wheels 4 ft. 6 in. in diameter, 16 in. by 24 in. cylinders, steam pressure 140 lb. per sq. in., a total heating surface of 756 sq. ft., and weighed $37\frac{1}{2}$ tons in working order. The first batch were known as Class "D" and were numbered 8, 11, 15, 16, 39 and 42. The second lot which were very slightly longer engines were known as Class "E" and numbered 37, 38 and 41. They are notable engines for the fact that they were the first tank engines in this country to be fitted with doors between the cab and the bunker. Mr. Manson was always very considerate of the welfare of the men under him and this was another example of his thoughtfulness for them, for the exclusion of draughts must have added greatly to the comfort of the drivers and firemen.

These little engines did a lot of useful work round Aberdeen on suburban and short distance traffic. At one time they also worked the Alford branch and later when the Fraserburgh to St. Combs light railway was opened one of them worked it. As that line was un-fenced the engine working it was fitted with a small cow catcher—surely a unique feature of British Rail-way working! At the end of their lives they were mostly employed on the Waterloo Branch and shunt-ing at Kittybrewster. They were all rebuilt by Mr. Pickersgill between 1907 and 1911. He fitted them with larger boilers having—with the firebox—a heat-ing surface of 846 sq. ft. and a pressure of 150 lb. per sq. in. He also gave them chimneys and boiler mount-ings of his standard design, and in their new shape they looked very sturdy little engines. As so rebuilt the "D" Class weighed 42 tons and the "E" Class 43 tons 5 cwt. All passed to the L. and N.E. at the amal-gamation and were scrapped by them between 1931 and 1935.

In 1887 Mr. Manson achieved the remarkable feat of building two engines at Kittybrewster. As there was only room for four engines in the erecting shop and as a lot of the work had to be done outside this was a very creditable effort. It will be remembered that the Chairman told the shareholders that they ex-pected to save between £300 and £400 by building these engines themselves instead of getting them built outside. The engines were very similar to Nos. 69-71, but they had 5 ft. 7 in. coupled wheels. To com-

G.N. of S.R. Locomotive No. 38, Class "E."

G.N. of S.R. Locomotive No. 18, Class "O."

memorate the fact that they were "home made" they were given names as well as numbers. No. 5 was called " Kilmundy " after the Chairman's home and No. 6 " Thomas Adam " after the deputy Chairman. These names were painted straight across the front splashers and were carried by the engines for some years, but were ultimately painted out by Mr. Pickersgill.

All these earlier Manson tender engines survived after rebuilding long enough to be taken over by the L. & N.E., but it cannot be said that they had a particularly distinguished career.

The coming of express trains on the main line called for something more powerful and to work them Mr. Manson next designed some very useful and interesting locomotives. Nine of them were built by Messrs. Kitson in 1888. They were known as Class "O" and were numbered 4, 7, 9, 10, 17, 18, and 72-74. Their cylinders were 18 in. by 26 in. The slide valves were placed above the cylinders and worked by rocking shafts, which arrangement permitted the use of unusually large bogie wheels with a diameter of 3 ft. $9\frac{1}{2}$ in. They were one of the earliest examples of express engines in this country to be fitted with a modern form of rocking shaft. The bogies were of the swing link type having double pins, and were also interesting as being almost the first swing link bogies to be fitted to any engines in Great Britain. The coupled wheels were 6 ft. $0\frac{1}{2}$ in. in diameter. The boilers were 4 ft. 4 in. in diameter and had 1,094 sq. ft. of heating surface, to which the firebox added 106 sq. ft., making a total of 1,200 sq. ft. The grate area was 18 sq. ft. and the working pressure 150 lb. per sq. in. In working order the engine weighed 42 tons, of which 28 tons 18 cwt. were available for adhesion. Six wheeled tenders were provided weighing 34 tons 10 cwt. in working order and having a water capacity of 3,000 gallons and carrying 3 tons of coal. It is interesting to note that Mr. Manson had continued Mr. Clark's air inlets in the firebox though in a modified form. They were 3 in. in diameter and placed at the front and back of the fire boxes instead of at the sides. The steam nozzles were discarded for the blower was found to be quite efficient in maintaining the air currents when steam was shut off.

Two of these engines, Nos. 18 and 74, were involved in a head-on collision at Huntly two years after they were built. There was then no interlocking of signals and points there and the two trains were allowed on the same set of rails by the mistake of the pointsman. Fortunately only a few people were injured and not much damage was done as one train was standing and the other only moving slowly at the time of the collision.

Three more engines of the same type came from Messrs. R. Stephenson & Co. in 1890. Tenders of a new type were fitted to them, having eight wheels of which the leading pair were bogie and the back pair rigid. These rather odd looking tenders weighed 36 tons and carried 3,000 gallons of water and 3¼ tons of coal. They were the first eight-wheeled tenders to be fitted to any engines in this country. The engines were numbered 12-14 and were known as Class "P".

In the same year the same builders delivered three more engines having the same general dimensions and

G.N. of S.R. Locomotive No. 13, Class "P."

By courtesy of Major S. A. Forbes.

eight wheel tenders but with 6 ft. 6½ in. coupled wheels
—the largest ever given to a Great North engine. They
formed Class "Q" and bore the numbers 75-77. No. 77
was rebuilt in 1914 by Mr. Pickersgill with a superheater and was the first Great North engine to be fitted
with one. No. 76 was rebuilt at the same time but
without the superheater and tests were made between
the two engines to determine the relative merits of
superheated and saturated steam under the working
conditions of the Great North. The superheater won
and most of these last three Classes of Mr. Manson's
engines were rebuilt with superheaters in consequence. As rebuilt No. 77 was fitted with a boiler
4 ft. 6 in. in diameter and 10 ft. 10½ in. between tube
plates. The tubes gave 448 sq. ft. of heating surface
and the flues 242 sq. ft. The superheater consisted
of eighteen elements 1 3/32 in. in diameter giving 140
sq. ft. of heating surface. The firebox had a grate area
of 18.2 sq. ft. and gave 106 sq. ft. heating surface.
Steam pressure was 160 lb. per sq. in. No. 76 had a
total heating surface of 1,165 sq. ft. and a working
pressure of 160 lb. per sq. in. Cylinders in both
engines remained 18 in. by 26 in. No. 77 weighed
47 tons and No. 76 one ton less. After rebuilding
No. 77 was put on all the hardest trains including the
Mail, which was probably the hardest of any on the
system, and this she worked with considerable success.

All the other engines of Classes "O", "P" and "Q"
were rebuilt between 1915 and 1920 by Mr. Heywood.
Nos. 17, 18, 72-74 of Class "O", Nos. 12 and 14 of
Class "P", and No. 75 of Class "Q" were given boilers
with superheaters similar to that of No. 77, while Nos.
4, 7, 9 and 10 of Class "O" and 13 of Class "P" had

boilers similar to No. 76. In almost all cases the eight-wheeled tenders were replaced by standard six-wheeled tenders. When these engines were rebuilt, No. 77 had a modified cab, the roof being carried further back and was supported by pillars, but all the others retained their original cabs.

In 1890 Mr. Manson returned to the Glasgow and South Western Railway as its Locomotive Superintendent. He left some very useful engines on the Great North, but his great achievement was the automatic tablet exchanger which has already been described. During his superintendency some enlargements and improvements were made at the Kittybrewster works but they were still too small, particularly for building engines, and probably the saving in cost which he achieved on the two he managed to build there was one of the reasons for the transfer of the works to Inverurie, which was decided on a few years after he left.

His successor was Mr. James Johnson, who came from Derby and was a son of Mr. S. W. Johnson who was at that time Locomotive Superintendent of the Midland Railway. He was only at Kittybrewster for four years but designed two Classes of Locomotives, one of which became virtually the standard type for the future and the other was one of the most useful types the railway ever possessed. This latter class consisted of nine 0-4-4 tank engines known as Class "R" and numbered 84-92. They were expressly built for work on the Deeside line and for some years after their advent were limited to that section. For several years they worked regularly right through to Ballater though after about the beginning of the present cen-

G.N. of S.R. Locomotive No. 90, Class "R."

G.N. of S.R. Locomotive No. 78, Class "S."   *By courtesy of Major S. A. Forbes.*

tury they were confined to the suburban and semi-suburban services. One of them also usually worked on the Cruden Bay line for by the time it was opened they were allowed on to the Buchan route. But their life's work was really on the Aberdeen suburban services. As has been seen, the timings of all these trains were very "tight" and these engines made a great reputation for themselves for the smart way in which they worked them. Their principal dimensions were as follows: Coupled wheels 5 ft. 1 in. diameter; bogie wheels 3 ft. 0½ in. in diameter. The cylinders had a bore of 17½ in. and a stroke of 26 in. The boilers, which had a mean diameter of 4 ft. 5 in., gave a heating surface of 1,093.5 sq. ft. and the fireboxes 113.5, making a total of 1,207 sq. ft. The grate area was 18.26 sq. ft. and the working pressure 165 lb. per sq. in. The weight in working order was 53 tons.

Mr. Johnson's other type were 4-4-0 tender engines known as Class "S" and numbered 78-83. They were a distinct advance on anything the Great North had and were admirably suited to its requirements. They had the same sized bogie wheels as Mr. Manson's engines—3 ft. 9½ in. in diameter—but the coupled wheels were slightly larger at 6 ft. 1 in. Their boilers and fireboxes were similar to those of the tank engines just described and they had the same working pressure —165 lb. per sq. in. Their weight in working order was 43 tons 18 cwt. The tenders had six wheels 4 ft. 1 in. in diameter and had a capacity for 3 tons of coal and 3,000 gallons of water. The weight was 35 tons in working order, making a total for engine and tender of 78 tons 18 cwt. Both these types were built by Messrs. Neilson & Co. of Glasgow in 1893.

As Mr. Johnson had such close connections with the Midland it was not surprising that his engines had several characteristics in common with that Company's engines. The chimneys were very similar to those of the Midland and the safety valves were placed on the top of the domes though the spring balances which were so characteristic of Midland practice were omitted. But the Midland's neat brass column on the firebox duly appeared on the Great North engines.

Mr. Johnson resigned in 1894 and was succeeded by Mr. William Pickersgill, who came from the Great Eastern. At that time the Great Eastern rolling stock was probably the most hideous of any in Great Britain, but luckily the new locomotive superintendent brought none of its peculiarities with him. In fact he proceeded to design some of the best looking rolling stock in Scotland and by the end of the century the Great North's expresses were hard to beat for appearance as well as comfort.

The middle 'nineties was a period of rapid expansion of the train services and more locomotives were necessary soon after the new Superintendent came. To meet this need he designed a type of 4-4-0 which was really a further edition of Mr. Johnson's engines with various alterations of detail, the most noticeable of which was the abolition of the particularly Midland characteristics. The safety valves were removed from the dome and the brass column on the firebox was replaced by an enclosed Ramsbottom safety valve. The principal dimensions, however, remained the same. With this type, which are known as Class "T", the old "rule of three" which had governed the number

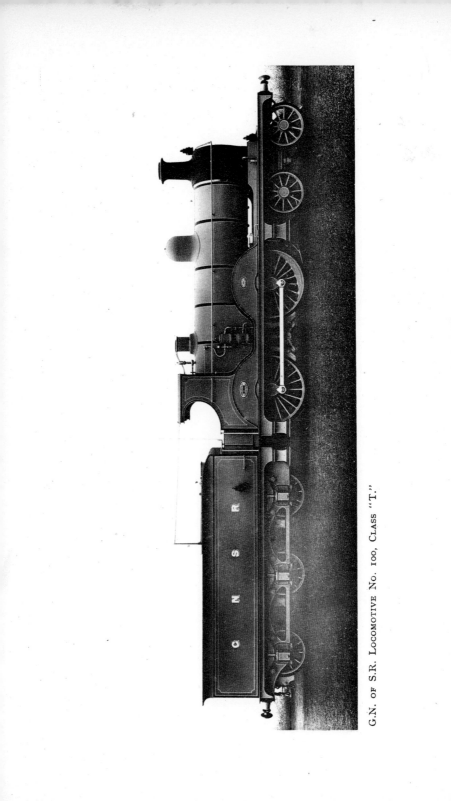

G.N. of S.R. Locomotive No. 100, Class "T."

of engines of any one type was at last broken and
no less than twenty-six of these engines were built.
They were delivered as follows :

93—99	in 1895 (Neilson & Co.)
100 & 19-24	in 1896 (Neilson & Co.)
101—106	in 1897 (Neilson & Co.)
107—112	in 1898 (Neilson, Reid & Co.)

To these engines fell the task of working the greatly
improved services which were instituted in the spring
of 1897 and this they carried out with complete success. Despite the comparatively small size of their
coupled wheels they were capable of running at high
speeds and the late Rev. W. J. Scott recorded that on
one occasion he timed one to cover a mile in 45.2
secs. = 79.66 m.p.h.   As the first three-quarters of that
mile were down hill at a gradient of 1 in 100 and the
last quarter was on the level it is not unreasonable to
presume than 80 m.p.h. was reached or exceeded.
High speed could always be looked for on the falling
grades south of Kennethmont, and the same author-
ity records a run in which the $26\frac{1}{2}$ miles from passing
Kennethmont to the stop at Dyce were covered in
23 minutes 46 seconds.   There is a story that Aberdeen was once reached in 39 minutes from Huntly.
Though this is unconfirmed it is on record that on
one occasion when the 10.32 a.m. from Elgin was de-
layed in starting till after 11 a.m. the run was made in
less than 2 hours with 9 stops—Dyce being passed on
this occasion.   The loads, of course, in those days
were light.

Later in their history these engines were still capable of very smart work   One day in July 1912 when

the Mail was run in two portions No. 95 worked
the Craigellachie portion and a load of 135 tons, from
Cairnie Junction to Huntly—7½ miles of which 4 of the
last 5 are uphill mostly between 1 in 120 and 1 in 180
—in 9 min. 27 secs. The 8 uphill miles from Huntly
to Kennethmont took only 11 m. 6 s. Insch (12¼
miles) was passed in 16 m. 8 s., and despite two checks
after that Inveramsay (20¼ miles) was reached in the
smart time of 23 m. 16 s. Another good start was
made from Inverurie, Pitmedden 8½ miles out being
passed in 9 m. 53 s., but after that several signal delays occurred. On a previous occasion the same
engine took a load of 230 tons from Huntly to Dyce
in 43½ m., the 16 miles from Kennethmont to Inverurie being covered in just under 15 m., despite the
slack through Inveramsay which was severe on this
occasion.

When the Deeside express was quickened in 1914
some smart running was often done by these engines
working it. On one occasion No. 103 took 190 tons
from Banchory to Aberdeen (16¾ miles) in 20 m. 28
secs., the bare 14 miles from Crathes to Hollum Street
being covered in 13 minutes 32 seconds. On another
occasion No. 93 with the down train covered the 23¾
miles from Aberdeen to Torphins in 30 m. 1 sec. with
a load of 160 tons to Banchory and 120 from there.
Banchory was passed in 21 m. 52 sec., and the 7 miles
from there, including 3½ miles of a rising gradient of
1 in 70, took only 8 min. 9 secs. These were both very
smart runs for going down in addition to the heavy
gradients west of Banchory there is a four mile bank
at the start which includes a short stretch at 96 be-

fore Ferryhill and $1\frac{1}{4}$ miles at 101 from the $1\frac{3}{4}$ mile post. Up trains have a severe check at Ferryhill.

In 1899 an order for ten more locomotives was placed with Messrs. Neilson, Reid & Co. but by the time they came to be delivered it had been found necessary to reduce the train mileage and so many engines were not required.   Five were accordingly sold to the South Eastern and Chatham Railway who were at that time short of engines, and they became their Nos. 676-680. The five kept by the Great North were given the numbers 113-115, 25 and 26. These engines were known as the "V" Class and had the same principal dimensions as the previous class but differed from them in having square cabs with side windows and a raised ventilator in the roof. They were certainly among the best looking small engines ever built.

The Great North's stud of locomotives had now reached its maximum number, which was only reached again at the very end of its life. In addition to the 115 capital engines there were at that time 10 engines on the duplicate list at work, the two original tank engines No. 13A and 14A and eight of the last design of 2-4-0's Nos. 19A to 26A. No. 27 of that series was still on the capital list and so remained till she was broken up in 1909. (The others had all gone by then, the first to go being No. 20A which was broken up in December 1900 and the last Nos. 21A, 22A, 25A and 26A which went in 1907.) By the end of the nineteenth century, therefore, the Great North was thoroughly well equipped with engines, all of which were very well looked after and kept always in first class condition. They could certainly not have performed the work they did had that not been so, nor could they have lasted so well. That so many of them lasted so long as they did—few, if any, failed to last 40 years—speaks volumes for the way they had been built and maintained.

The Great North locomotive stock had one outstanding peculiarity—there were no goods engines. This was not, of course, due to the fact that there were no goods trains, for there were plenty of them, but rather to the circumstances of the railway. By having engines which could go anywhere and do anything that was reasonably likely to be asked of them considerable economies were made possible. Fewer types allowed a greater degree of standardisation and also simplified the working arrangements, thereby reducing light engine mileage to a minimum. The Great North could never afford to disregard any reasonable form of economy!

In the early years of the present century steam rail motor cars became fashionable on a good many railways, and the Great North decided to try them. Two were accordingly built in 1905 which had several features of interest. The engines were supplied by Messrs. A. Barclay, Sons & Co., and were fitted with special vertical boilers made by Messrs. Cochran of Annan—the first time these Cochran boilers were applied to railway work. They were 9 ft. 6 in. high and 6 ft. in diameter, and contained 295 horizontal return fire tubes 3 ft. 11½ in. long and 1½ in. diameter. Their tops were dome-shaped which gave these rail-cars a very odd appearance. The heating surface was 500 sq. ft., the grate area 9 sq. ft. and the working pres-

sure 150 lb. per square inch. The engines had two
horizontal cylinders 10 in. in diameter with a stroke
of 16 in. and they drove the leading wheels of the
bogie, which were 3 ft. 7 in. in diameter. Walschaert
valve gear was provided. The water was carried in
a tank having a capacity of 600 gallons, which was
hung under the body of the carriage. The body was
built at Inverurie and had seating accommodation for
45 passengers on garden chairs arranged on either
side of an open saloon 34 ft. 7 in. long. There was
also a small end compartment by which passengers
entered and left the car and which was also the driver's
when running carriage first. The overall length was
49 ft. 11½ in. and the approximate weight in working
order and with a full complement of passengers 47
tons. On its trial one of them reached a speed of 60
miles an hour and attained 30 miles an hour in 20
seconds. They were given the locomotive numbers
29 and 31, so replacing the first of the original 4-4-0's
to be broken up.

They were tried on the Aberdeen suburban services
and on the Lossiemouth and St. Combs branches, but
were a complete failure, as their boilers proved inadequate and they were very noisy. After two years
they were broken up into their component parts, the
bodies being converted into rather short bogie third-
class saloons and the engines into tank engines. They
did not survive long in this shape being replaced by
two tender engines which took their numbers in the
autumn of 1909 and early part of 1910.

These two engines were part of a new series of Class
"V" engines—the first of which, No. 27, was built at

Inverurie in 1909 and was thus the first engine to be built there. The others were No. 29 also built in 1909, Nos. 31 and 36 built in 1910, Nos. 28 and 33 built in 1913, No. 35 built in 1914, and No. 34 built in 1915, making eight in all. They were all built at Inverurie.

In 1914 Mr. Pickersgill left to become Locomotive Superintendent of the Caledonian Railway—a position which he held till the amalgamation. His superintendency of the Great North rolling stock had been an eventful one. The planning and building of the new works at Inverurie had been his; he built or rebuilt 79 locomotives out of a total stock of 115 and revolutionised the passenger stock. Great North rolling stock was always well looked after and his reign was no exception to this for he maintained and left it in absolutely first class condition.

Mr. T. E. Heywood came from the Taff Vale to succeed him, but almost before he had had a chance to look round the War came. He built the last of the above-mentioned "V" Class engines in 1915 and in the same year the railway took over the working of the traffic at Aberdeen Harbour and for this four small tank engines were procured from Messrs. Manning, Wardle & Co. They were of two types, the first of which had 4 ft. coupled wheels, 14 in. by 20 in. cylinders and 140 lb. steam pressure. They were at first numbered 116 and 117, but these numbers were changed later to 30 and 32 * thus replacing the last of the original 4-4-0's. These, however, were not broken up till 1917. The other two new engines were slightly smaller, having 3 ft. 6 in. wheels and 13 in. by 20 in. cylinders. They were numbered 43 and 44.

---

*See illustration facing page 38.

G.N. of S.R. Steam Railcar No. 29.

G.N. of S.R. Locomotive No. 27, Class "V."
(The first built at Inverurie.)

No more engines were built till after the War, so
Mr. Heywood's main line engines did not appear till
1920. These were a superheated edition of the "V"
Class and were known as Class "F". The boilers had
the same diameter as the earlier engines, but the heating surface was differently arranged. There were 204
tubes 1¾ in. in diameter and 18 superheater tubes of
4¾ in. in diameter, giving a heating surface of 512 and
242 sq. ft. respectively. The superheater heating surface was 140 sq. ft. The firebox had a grate area of
18.26 sq. ft. and a heating surface of 106 sq. ft. Steam
pressure was 160 lb. per sq. in. They had cylinders
18 in. in diameter with a stroke of 26 in., coupled
wheels 6 ft. 1 in. and bogie wheels 3 ft. 9½ in. in diam.
and weighed 46 tons 19 cwt., of which 33 tons 4 cwt.
were available for adhesion. The tenders had 6 wheels
4 ft. 1 in. in diameter and carried 5 tons of coal and
3,000 gallons of water.

During the War Mr. Heywood had changed the
colour of the engines from green, which in one shade
or another had been the standard Great North colour
from the first, to black picked out with yellow and
lined with red. These new engines were painted in
this style and looked very smart. Their appearance was greatly improved by having the
Company's coat of arms emblazoned on the
front splashers. Another new feature was that
they were all named, the names being carried on a
neat brass plate round the top of the front splasher.
Six of these engines were built by the North British
Locomotive Company and were delivered at the end of
1920. Their names and numbers were as follows :

o

47 Sir David Stewart.   50 Hatton Castle.
48 Andrew Bain.   52 Glen Grant.
49 Gordon Highlander.   54 Southesk.

During the coal strike of 1921 No. 49 was fitted for burning oil fuel, but the apparatus was removed soon after the end of the strike.

Two more engines of the same type were built at Inverurie in 1921—No. 45 "George Davidson" and No. 46 "Benachie" and this latter was the last locomotive built for the old Great North.

As there were no engines withdrawn after that the Great North total locomotive stock stood at the end of its life as 125 of which 103 were 4-4-0 tender engines, 9 were 0-6-0 tank engines, 9 0-4-4 tank engines and 4 0-4-2 tank engines. A full list of these is given in the appendix.

Though the Great North's early passenger carriages were described as "elegant and commodious" by a contemporary reporter, and the fact that its third-class coaches were externally indistinguishable from its first-class ones was a matter of pride to its chairman, it cannot be denied that they were small and rather box-like affairs. The thirds, too, were really "whited sepulchres" for, despite their external resemblance to the firsts, internally they were provided with no partitions and, of course, no upholstery. A characteristic which remained with them all their lives was the "guard's seat" on the roof. They were, of course, all four-wheelers—not that that fact was necessarily against them, for the addition of a pair of

G.N. OF S.R. LOCOMOTIVE No. 54.

By courtesy of the North British Locomotive Co. Ltd.

wheels often only meant an additional point of wheel-jolt! Why six-wheelers should have been so popular in this country has always been a mystery to the author, for there were plenty of longer coaches on the continent on only four wheels and the presence of an extra pair was far from meaning additional comfort to the traveller. Be that as it may, the Great North in due course followed the fashion and six-wheelers made their appearance at a later date.

There was not much improvement—if any—in the stock till the sweeping changes which took place in the 'eighties. The new carriages which then appeared were a great improvement on the old ones, being altogether bigger and roomier and having an attractive interior. In one respect some of them were quite in line with what is to-day considered the most modern practice—namely, their windows were set flush with the extreme ouside line of the coach— but this was confined to comparatively few of them.

The greatest changes, however, took place after Mr. Pickersgill's appointment as Locomotive and Carriage and Wagon Superintendent. In 1896 he introduced corridor carriages which must have been the first of their kind built for any *purely* Scottish service. They were of three types—first-class having four compartments, first and third composites, having two first and three third class compartments, and third class having five compartments. Each type had two lavatories side by side across the carriage, one of which served one compartment and the other the rest in the case of the first and third class coaches, while in the composite one served the first and one the third class. All the end compartments were the full width of the coach. Electric light was provided—the Great North never used gas. It was a pity that they ran on six wheels and not on bogies, but this is hardly surprising when one remembers that even the Royal Train consisted partly of six-wheelers in those days!

The appearance of these carriages was greatly improved by the new colour scheme introduced about this time. Previously the carriages had been painted a sombre brown, but the colour scheme now introduced was much more attractive. The lower panels were described as "purple lake" and the upper panels cream picked out with red and yellow. The whole effect was very pleasing and these colours remained the standard for passenger stock as long as Mr. Pickersgill remained in charge, and were only very slightly modified by his successor.

Two years later some very fine new bogie composites were built for working on the through Aberdeen to Inverness expresses. They were 48 ft. long over the body and contained two first and four third class compartments. The lavatories were at each end and provision was made for vestibule connections though these were only fitted to a few at that time. These carriages had one very attractive feature which was unique to themselves—separate ceilings were provided to the compartments and corridors, thus avoiding the lop-sided appearance common to most corridor stock. They were, of course, lit by electricity. Their weight was 25 tons and they were very smooth-running coaches. They were built at Kittybrewster and it says a lot for them that they continued to be

Early First and Third Class Composite Carriage.

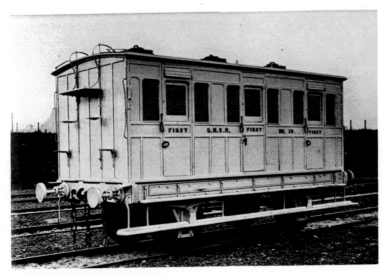

Early First Class Carriage.

used on the service for which they were built for many years after the Great North had become the London and North Eastern.

The Great North's traffic did not call for any special types of carriage, but in the possession of a Royal Saloon carriage they were alone among the Scottish railways. This carriage came out soon after the bogie composites had made their appearance and was often used for Royal travellers. It was 48 ft. long by 8 ft. 6 in. wide and was divided into two saloon compartments, one first class compartment and an attendant's coupé. The middle saloon could be converted for day or night use. By day it contained two sofas and four armchairs with two tables at the side; for night use the tables could be folded up and an armchair removed, so allowing room for a bed to be set up. The other saloon compartment was at the extreme end and people entered and left by it as the central saloon had no side door. Meals could be served if necessary from the attendant's coupé, which was fitted with a cooking stove. The lighting was electric and the carriage was heated by hot water circulation. Unlike all other Great North carriages, it had a clerestory roof, the clerestory being rather low and with square ends.

Railways are very prone to follow fashions and early in the present century clerestory roofs went out and high elliptical ones came in. This fashion did not reach Inverurie in its more extreme form, but the coaches built from 1906 onwards had higher roofs than the earlier ones. Their appearance was also improved by the insertion of small lights above the windows. Some very fine carriages were built with these characteristics before the War, of which the most notable were some 54 ft. corridor vestibule first and third brake composites built for working through between Edinburgh and Glasgow and Elgin.

Mr. Pickersgill's last passenger rolling stock were some non-corridor six wheeled thirds, third brake composites and brake vans all of which were built to match the newest bogie stock externally and were very good riding vehicles.

After the War Mr. Heywood added some non-corridor bogie thirds which were admirably adapted for the services for which they were built, and also some new bogie brake vans.

Two other interesting types of rolling stock remain to be mentioned. The first of these were some Bicycle vans which were introduced at the beginning of the century when the bicycling rage was at its height. They were "double-deckers", one lot of bicycles being carried in a row of compartments on the lower floor with another row above them. They were very useful at that time but as motors took the place of bicycles they were converted into carriage trucks.

The other type of rolling stock was a ballast train built at about the same time. It consisted of "hopper" type wagons for carrying ballast from which it could be emptied straight on to the track. The brake van was fitted with a plough which levelled the ballast so deposited as the train moved on. This was an early application of a principle which is now commonly used.

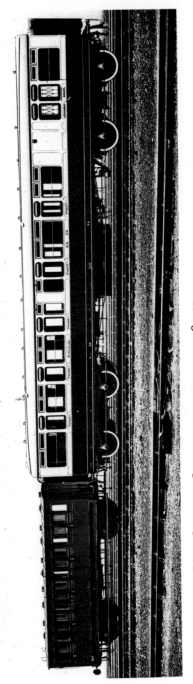

G.N. of S.R. 54FT. BOGIE COMPOSITE CARRIAGE ATTACHED TO OLD COACH.

CHAPTER TEN.

THE WAR—AND THE END.

THE year nineteen hundred and fourteen marked the close of an epoch in British Railway History. On the outbreak of War all the railways were taken over by the Government and though they were handed back to their owners when hostilities were over the period which followed was an uneasy interval spent in repairing the damages done by the four years of strife and preparing for the amalgamations decided on by Parliament.

The outbreak of War found the Great North of Scotland in very good condition—which was as well, for during the War years heavy extra burdens were put on it.

The concentration of the Fleet at Scapa Flow caused a serious transport problem. The harbour nearest to the Fleet was Scrabster, but it was far too small to deal with the traffic and was two and a half miles from the Railway at Thurso. Moreover, Thurso was at the extreme end of the Highland line and most of the two hundred and seventy-two miles of railway which connected Thurso with Perth were single and likely to be very fully occupied. An alternative was offered by Aberdeen where there was a good harbour which was well served by rail and where also there was ample siding accommodation for the Cale-

donian Railway's new sidings at Craiginches, just
South of Aberdeen, could hold six hundred trucks.
Aberdeen was therefore chosen as the distribution
centre for the Grand Fleet as from January 15th, 1915.

The Naval traffic was concentrated on the North
West side of the Victoria Dock where there was an
admirable transit shed. The War had stopped most
of the commercial traffic between Aberdeen and the
Continent so this could readily be made available. The
method of handling the trucks was that they were
stopped and marshalled at Craiginches and sent on
from there as ordered by the Admiralty, thus avoiding congestion in the goods stations and at the docks.
Their contents were taken to the Fleet by coasting
steamers of which there were eight in regular service.
Everything required for the Grand Fleet and its bases
was shipped from Aberdeen, including "fifty sea-
planes, a hundred motor lorries and cars, ten locomotives, twelve travelling cranes, all classes of guns and
munitions up to 6 in., all classes of boats (steam,
motor, sailing and pulling) up to a length of sixty feet,
about six hundred thousand gallons of lubricating oil,
one hundred and fifty thousand gallons of petrol and
five hundred thousand sacks of potatoes." Also fifty
thousand tons of cement! A good mixed bag! In
addition to the general stores there were the victual-
ling stores for the Fleet which in one month (October
1918) amounted to eight hundred and seventy-eight
tons.

In 1915 the Great North of Scotland took over the
working of the traffic on the docks and, as has been
seen in the last chapter, bought four tank engines
especially for this work. The Admiralty work con-

tinued after the War was over and between January
15th, 1915, and February 28th, 1919, the Great North
Railway worked on Admiralty account sixty-seven
thousand eight hundred and twenty-three loaded
wagons between their own goods yard and those of
the Caledonian and North British Railways and the
Aberdeen harbour. The estimated weight of their
contents was two hundred and ninety-seven thousand
nine hundred tons. The average six monthly volume
of traffic handled was thirty-five thousand tons,
the heaviest period being the first half of 1918
when fifty thousand tons were dealt with. This vast
work was carried out with complete smoothness and
to the entire satisfaction of the Admiralty, one of
whose representatives "spoke in terms of the highest
praise of the cordial and ever willing assistance rendered to them by the Railway and Harbour Officials
at Aberdeen".

Peterhead Harbour was used for bunkering mine
sweepers and other vessels.   For this purpose the
railway carried over its Buchan line sixteen thousand
and eighty-seven tons of Welsh, and seventy-two
thousand and eighteen tons of Scottish coal, a total
of eighty-eight thousand one hundred and five tons.
The Admiralty had established an Airship Station at
Lenabo about three and a half miles from Longside
Station also on the Buchan section, and the Railway
built a line to it and carried a total of thirty-one
thousand nine hundred and thirteen tons there.

In many parts of the North East of Scotland and
particularly on Deeside and Strathspey there was a
large amount of timber, much of which was cut for
war purposes—chiefly sleepers for use at home and

in France and for pitprops. The Canadian Forestry Corps had camps at Kemnay, Knockando and Nethybridge. At one time German prisoners were also employed on this work. From all over the system there was an enormous output of timber and in 1918 the railway carried two hundred and thirty-eight thousand tons which compared with a total of fifty-one thousand seven hundred and ninety-seven in 1913.

Another normal traffic which was increased enormously by war conditions was herrings. As there was no export trade in herrings during the War they had all to be carried inland by rail. In 1918 fifty-three thousand three hundred and two tons of fresh herrings were carried by the Great North, an increase of no less than forty-six thousand two hundred and fifteen tons on the total for 1913! Moreover, the War closed the ports round the North East Coast and so much traffic which was sea-borne in peace time had to go by rail during the War. It is not known exactly how much this traffic amounted to, but it was estimated at fifty thousand tons a year.

These were very large increases of traffic for a small railway and the Great North war work was not confined to traffic to and from its own system. Even though Aberdeen was the chief distributing centre for the Grand Fleet much traffic for it had also to be carried over the Highland Railway and they had to handle the whole of the traffic for naval requirements at Invergordon, which were enormous. Pressure on the Highland line was therefore intense, and the Great North proved a very valuable alternative route. Altogether they took forty-eight thousand four hundred and forty loaded and nine thousand and thirty-three empty wagons to and from Highland stations which would normally have gone down the Highland main line. They were also able to help in another way, and during the War their engines ran a total of half a million miles on Highland railway metals. Frequently, too, naval ambulance trains had to be taken from the Highland system at short notice.

The Works at Inverurie were also used for the manufacture of a variety of things for war use and they provided seventy transport wagons, three hundred and fifty pick and fencing posts, three thousand five hundred pegs, sixty-four thousand and ninety adaptors for Grays Fuse No. 100, twelve hundred and seventeen greenade dischargers, twenty-four regulation ambulance stretchers and four snow ploughs for use in France—a truly miscellaneous collection.

Though the Great North were never called upon to send any rolling stock for actual war service they provided a train of thirty-one passenger coaches during the period of demobilisation which was sent to France on January 17th, 1919, and returned home at the end of the following March. Immediately on the outbreak of War, in circumstances of great emergency, they also provided an ambulance train for use at home. Later on they provided two passenger train vans which were fitted up as naval ambulance vans. These were used by the Admiralty and also frequently by the Red Cross Society for conveying wounded men to and from convalescent homes.

In all, six hundred and nine members of the staff fought in one war theatre or another. Of these ninety-three never returned and many others were wounded. Three members of the staff were awarded the Military Cross and three the Distinguished Conduct Medal, while nineteen were given the Military Medal (one of whom also gained a bar), and one the Meritorious Service Medal. Two of those who received the Military Medal were also awarded the Belgian Croix de Guerre, and two were also mentioned in Despatches. In addition to the number of men who actually served in the Forces, a squad consisting of one Assistant Engineer, one Permanent Way Inspector, five Foremen and thirty-nine Platelayers were sent to France in March, 1917, and remained there till about the end of June.

To commemorate those who had fallen, a memorial tablet with a list of their names was erected in the Company's Offices. The Company set aside the sum of £2,000, the interest on which was to be used to assist the dependents of their employees who had been killed. It was proposed that when the necessity for this had ended the interest should be earmarked for the assistance of men who met with accidents during the course of their regular work, and possibly to encourage the educational equipment of the Company's employees.

At the end of the War a great many schemes were considered for making a better and brighter Britain, one of which was the improvement of transport facilities in Scotland. Early in 1918 a Committee was appointed by the Secretary of State for Scotland "to consider and report upon: (a) the rural areas in Scotland which are most in need of transport facilities for the promotion of agriculture, forestry and other rural industries, and (b) the means of improving communication in these areas with special reference to new or improved roads, light and narrow gauge railways and motor transport, including any consequential modification of existing steamer services." This Committee made a full examination of the area served by the Great North of Scotland Railway, and considered a number of schemes for light railways which had been proposed in the past. There was considerable local demand at that time for the construction of a number of light railways, motor transport being then looked upon as a means of building up traffic which could later be served by the construction of a light railway, and this view was also taken by the Commission. In the end they recommended the construction of four railways namely, from Ballater to Braemar, from Alford to Strathdon, from Turriff to Maud, and from Fraserburgh to New Aberdour, the latter, if connection with the existing railway could be made at a reasonable cost. Amongst other schemes considered were those for a railway from Aberdeen to Echt and Aberdeen to Newburgh. For these routes, however, they recommended that the traffic should be continued to be handled by motor transport, but as in those days the art of making roads sufficiently strong to bear such heavy traffic had not been found, they proposed that a special concrete road should be laid alongside the existing roads to carry this traffic.

None of these schemes was ever carried out. The day of light railways had passed and concrete roads became unnecessary as ordinary roads improved. After the War the Government had a large number of lorries which had been used for military purposes, which they then sold, and this gave a tremendous fillip to motor transport. There is no doubt that the change to road transport was also hastened by the railway strike of 1920. This strike and that of 1926 did a great deal to damage the railway industry, for they taught the public that there were other and perhaps more dependable methods of transport, and they also antagonised a large number of people. What the men began the management continued. For nearly ten years after amalgamation, no serious effort was made to meet the new competition or to improve their relationships with the general public. When this policy was changed, and an era of great progress commenced it was too late. It is much easier to retain custom than to regain it.

The domestic affairs of the Great North of Scotland Railway in the years immediately following the War were influenced largely by the effects of the War and prospect of the coming amalgamation. War time traffic had put a severe strain on the rolling stock, and in common with those of all other railways the train services suffered in consequence. There was a shortage of locomotives, and to make this good, some engines were borrowed for a short time from the Great Central Railway. These were old Sacré four-coupled machines, and they returned unregretted to their old home when Mr. Heywood's new engines appeared. Coming events cast their shadows before, and in 1922 a restaurant car was borrowed from the North British Railway and put to working between Aberdeen and Inverness, leaving Aberdeen on the morning train as a breakfast car and returning as a

luncheon car on the mid-day train from Inverness.
In 1919 Sir David Stewart was succeeded as Chair-
man by Mr. Andrew Bain, who retired two years later
in favour of Mr. Alexander Duffus, who became the
Great North's representative on the Board of the
London and North Eastern Railway.

The rest of the story is soon told. Parliament had
decided that to meet the new post-war conditions the
railways of the country must be amalgamated into four
strong groups. It had at first been intended that the
Scottish railways should make a group by themselves
but this produced a great outcry in Scotland,
which was not altogether surprising. Before the War
the Scottish railways had been run on cheaper lines
than the English, and in particular their wages had
been on a lower scale.   During the War, however,
hours of work and rates of pay had been standardised for the whole of Great Britain, and this standardisation obviously therefore would have imposed a
much heavier burden on the Scottish lines than the
English. There can be no doubt that such standardisation was logical from the men's point of view, for
there was no very obvious reason why a man who
drove an express train from, say, Carlisle to Glasgow,
should be paid less than the man who just brought it
through to Carlisle, but it would have had a disastrous
effect on Scottish Railways. Traders, too, feared that
rates would be raised so joined in the outcry which was
heard loudly in Parliament.

The proposal to unite the Scottish railways in one
group was therefore found to be untenable and was
abandoned in favour of a longitudinal system of

grouping of the Northern lines.   What was at first known as the Eastern Group was therefore formed, which consisted of the Great Northern, Great Central, Great Eastern, North Eastern, North British and Great North of Scotland Railways.

For sentimental reasons the passing of the old Great North was regretted by many. For many years it had served the district well and the story of its early misdeeds had been forgotten.   Indeed it had many times led the way and the number of innovations for which it was responsible was remarkable for so small a Company.   Nevertheless the grouping really came just in time to save it.   A railway which depended to such a large extent as the Great North on short distance traffic was bound to be very hard hit by the new motor competition. There would have been a grim irony in its destruction by that very competitor which it had itself been the first to introduce into its own district!   While it therefore could not have stood alone much longer, as part of a larger group its system could continue to be of use to the district which it served.

The Act under which the Railways were amalgamated was passed in 1921 and came into force on 1st January, 1923, and so, with the passing of 1922, the Great North of Scotland Railway ceased to exist as a separate entity, being henceforth merged in the group which had come to be known as the London and North Eastern Railway.

Printed in Great Britain:
R. Tilling, 106 Great Dover Street, London, S.E.1.

APPENDIX.

Locomotives which passed from the Great North of Scotland Railway to the London and North Eastern Railway.

I. TENDER ENGINES (all 4-4-0):

(1) Class "K"   W. Cowan's 5 ft. 6½ in. class built 1866 (became L. & N.E.R. class "D47" part 2)
Nos. 44A, 45A, 48A   3 engines

(2) Class "L"   W. Cowan's 5 ft. 6½ in. class built 1876 (became L. & N.E.R. class "D47" part 1).
Nos. 49A, 50A, 52A, 54A, 55 & 56   6 engines

(3) Class "M"   W. Cowan's 5 ft. 7 in. class built 1878 (became L. & N.E.R class "D45")
Nos. 40, 51, 53, 57-62   9 engines

(4) Class "C"   W. Cowan's 6 ft. 1 in. class built 1879 (became L. & N.E.R. class "D39")
Nos. 1, 2 and 3   3 engines

(5) Class "A"   J. Manson's 6 ft. 0 in. class built 1884 (became L. & N.E.R. class "D44")
Nos. 63-68   6 engines

(6) Class "G"   J. Manson's 5 ft. 6 in. class built 1885 (became L. & N.E.R. class "D48")
Nos. 69-71   3 engines

(7) Class "H"   J. Manson's 5 ft. 7 in. class built 1887 (became L. & N.E.R class "D46")
Nos. 5 and 6   2 engines

(8) Class "O"   J. Manson's 6 ft. 0½ in. class built 1888 (became L. & N.E.R class "D42")
Nos. 4, 7, 9, 10 17, 18, 72-74. Of these Nos. 17, 18 and 72-74 had been rebuilt with superheaters, Nos. 4, 7, 9, 10 without.   9 engines

(9) Class "P"   J. Manson's 6 ft. 0½ in. class with eight-wheeled tenders built 1890 (became L. & N.E.R. class "D43").
Nos. 12, 13 and 14, of which Nos. 12 and 14 had been rebuilt with superheaters, No. 13 without.   3 engines

(10) Class "Q"   J. Manson's 6 ft. 6 in. class with eight-wheeled tenders built 1890 (became L. & N.E.R. class "D38").
Nos. 75-77. Nos. 75 and 77 rebuilt with superheaters, No. 76 without.   3 engines

(11) Class "S" J. Johnson's 6 ft. 1 in. class built 1893 (became L. & N.E.R. class "D41")
                     Nos. 78-83   6 engines

(12) Class "T" W. Pickersgill's 6 ft. 1 in. class built 1895-8 (became L. & N.E.R. class "D41").
         Nos. 19-24, 93-112   26 engines

(13) Class "V" W. Pickersgill's 6 ft. 1 in. class built 1899 and 1909-15, (became L. & N.E.R. class "D40").
  Nos. 25, 26, 113-115, 27-29, 31, 33-36   13 engines

(14) Class "F" T. E. Heywood's 6 ft. 1 in. superheated class built 1920-21 (became L. & N.E.R. class "D40").
         Nos. 45-50, 52 and 54   8 engines

        Total number of Tender Engines   ...   100

II. TANK ENGINES:

(1) Class "D" J. Manson's 0-6-0 type built 1884 (became L. & N.E.R. class "J90").
         Nos. 8, 11, 15, 16, 39, 42   6 engines

(2) Class "E" J. Manson's 0-6-0 type built 1885 (became L. & N.E.R. class "J91").
            Nos. 37, 38, 41   3 engines

(3) Class "Q" J. Johnson's 0-4-4 type built 1893 (became L. & N.E.R. class "G10").
            Nos. 84-92   9 engines

(4) Class "X" Manning, Wardle 0-4-2 3 ft. 6 in. class built 1915 (became L. & N.E.R. class "Z5" subsequently "Z4").
            Nos. 43 & 44   2 engines

(5) Class "Y" Manning, Wardle 0-4-2 4 ft. 0 in. class built 1915 (became L. & N.E.R. class "Z5").
          Nos. 30 and 32   2 engines

        Total number of Tank Engines ...   22
        Total number of all Engines   ...   122

NOTE.—When the L. & N.E.R. first started to re-number the engines of which it was made up it added a letter after the engines' original number, each railway having its own letter. For G.N.S. engines the letter was "S." Under the final scheme of re-numbering this was abolished and 6800 was added to all the old G.N.S. numbers.